ALMOST
HOME

GITHA HARIHARAN

ALMOST HOME

*Finding a Place in the World
from Kashmir to New York*

RESTLESS BOOKS
BROOKLYN, NEW YORK

In memory of Babu,
beloved brother by choice

Copyright © 2014 Githa Hariharan
First published in 2014 by Fourth Estate, an imprint of
HarperCollins Publishers India
Digital edition published by Restless Books, 2016
This edition published by Restless Books, 2016

Cover design by Nathan Burton
Cover photograph by Jasper James, printed with
permission from Millennium Images, UK.
Set in Garibaldi by Tetragon, London

Library of Congress Cataloging-in-Publication Data:
Available upon request.

ISBN: 978-1-63206-0-617

Printed in the United States of America

Ellison, Stavans, and Hochstein LP
232 3rd Street, Suite A111
Brooklyn, NY 11215
www.restlessbooks.com
publisher@restlessbooks.com

CONTENTS

Kublai Khan had noticed that Marco Polo's cities resembled one another, as if the passage from one to another involved not a journey but a change of elements. Now, from each city Marco described to him, the Great Khan's mind set out on its own, and after dismantling the city piece by piece, he reconstructed it in other ways, substituting components, shifting them, inverting them.

ITALO CALVINO
INVISIBLE CITIES

1

SEVEN CITIES AND ANYCITY

SEVEN CITIES, 1954–2012: MORE THAN ONE NATIVE

"What is your native?" This is a question all Indians are familiar with, having been asked by complete strangers on trains, or in bus queues, to reveal themselves with the name of a place. Further revelations may also be sought—about caste for instance, or marital status, or the number of blessings in the form of children, or monthly salary. But the soil you spring from is always the first step and the first stop.

The place could be a region. Knowing whether a person is South Indian or Bihari or Bengali is apparently of use to most Indian travelers. When you are going to live with someone in the intimacy of a train coach for two long days and one and a half nights, or even when you are going to sit for a half hour next to someone in a bus or metro, you have to decide whether you should give your new neighbor a wide berth or become a lifelong friend. Sometimes you may be treated to a reunion. Somehow, among the teeming millions, two people find they are relations—admittedly distant, possibly the daughter of the cousin of an uncle's brother-in-law. But what do a few degrees of separation matter when two people come from the same district or village or even the same street, and destiny in the shape of the Indian Railways or SpiceJet has brought them together?

Since chance is a tricky thing, your companion's native may not necessarily be a cause for celebration. In fact, in the crazy mix of India, most times it serves as a warning of difference; and every bit of received wisdom, however mythical, may be magically recalled.

There are also vast numbers of Indians who claim allegiance to a city. This, too, seems to offer the power of knowledge: people like us, people like them, or somewhere in between? When I was growing up, for instance, Bombay was Bombay and Delhi was Delhi and never the twain did meet.

But as with all hunger for knowledge, as with all thirst for classification, there is an exception—an exception that is not all that exceptional in India anymore. What do you do with a person who can't decide on her native? What if she is a natural or naturalized hybrid? A person with too many cities in her life, a person burdened by and enriched with too many natives?

* * *

I have lived all my life in a city, but if someone asked me, quite simply, "So which city are you from?" I wouldn't be able to answer. Or I would have too many answers: Bombay (this Bombay or that?); Manila; New York; Madras-Chennai; Bangalore-Bengaluru; Delhi. Or I could say: Anycity, composite city of visible cities, remembered cities, imagined cities.

But even a city-writer needs some sort of address, if only to pass on a message through the writing: please redirect; forward if necessary. In which case, my address should perhaps be Bombay because that's where my name and language got changed. (Later the city changed its name, too.)

Till the age of eight, I was called P.H. Githa and I studied in a school in which the medium of instruction was Tamil. My initials were very confident about where I came from. P for Perinkolam, literally Big Pond, was the village in Palghat my father came from. (Palghat used to be Palakkad, and has now gone back to being so, thanks to postcolonial corrective zeal.) H for Hariharan was the paterfamilias himself. My name mapped me geographically and patrilineally. It told the world I was Perinkolam Hariharan's Githa. More important, it told me who I was, where I came from, even what my place in the world was.

We didn't live in Palghat, though. We lived in Matunga, the South Indian stronghold of Bombay. In Matunga you could live a lifetime and lose little of your linguistic, culinary, and other assorted legacies to the host city. Then my father, a journalist, became the founder-editor of a newspaper, *The Economic Times*; and we moved from Matunga to Nepean Sea Road, not more than ten or twelve kilometers from South Indian School.

In Nepean Sea Road, a new world populated by Hindi, Marathi, and Gujarati speakers, but above all ruled by Indian English, unfolded for my bewilderment and delight. My sister and I practiced what we imagined was English. This English was a guttural, vowel-hating language; it made us happy because no one but the two of us understood it. But when we were sent to our new school, we discovered that the rest of the world, a place full of perverse people, spoke an English much less exciting (and much more exacting) than ours.

In my first week in the new school, an English-speaking little ogre, the class "monitor" and a boy several times my size, said to me: "Your name is PH? So your father's name must be Githa!" I did not need English—or his smirk—to understand that my stern all-knowing father was being reduced to a mere girl. My old self was due for a change. I was sent home with a note from my teacher demanding a "surname." Since we had no such thing, only the village initial and the father initial, my mother wrote my father's single name on a piece of paper. Hariharan. I was born again, this time without initials. My father was still there, but as a last name. I was no longer his alone. As for Perinkolam, the ancestral village, I lost it entirely. Tamil, too, was soon to be endangered, at least outside the home.

It occurs to me now that neither my parents nor my teachers were perturbed that I did not know a word of English. Apparently they knew something I didn't, because not long after I acquired a surname, the English followed quite meekly. In a year's time, I had learned the language that went with my new cosmopolitan name which would make it easier to fill out international application forms that took you places. The kind that begin, "First name? Family name?" I was not to know till many years later that I had been selected to become one of Macaulay's step/illegitimate great-grandchildren.

* * *

So two cities in my address already, Matunga-Bombay and Bombay. But before I could stay on and become a daughter of the soil, a Mumbaikar, I was transported to another city by the sea, Manila.

My Manila was the expat community (all best friends Pakistanis, though our countries were inching towards war), and the sea by Roxas Boulevard (not a patch on Marine Drive). Manila added Spanish and Tagalog to the pungent *khichdi* of Tamil, English, Marathi, Hindi, and "French" I had brought with me from Bombay. Manila was the Roman Catholic school I went to (Colegio de la Asunción, referred to as just Assumption), a place where I acquired a bit of everything, from liberal doses of Thomas Aquinas to *Madame Butterfly* to the best way to dance the tarantella and the French minuet. My incompetence in dance class was not the only thing that told me, once again, that I was different, and that in this city it was not just a question of language. In Manila I learned I was *Indian*. I was the only foreign student in class, and would I please immediately explain the caste system and the transmigration of souls to my thirty thirteen-year-old classmates? There's nothing like a child's clear-eyed deconstruction of the golden past to confirm the suspicion that it is nothing to boast about. Besides, there seemed to be a subtle, diabolic alliance between this *having to be Indian* with the nuns' *young ladies*. Consider, for example, the relationship between "Fourteen-year-old girls going to a party at night with boys? That's not Indian!" with "Girls, you are now young ladies. Which means you must always sit with your knees firmly together. And when you go down the stairs in your school skirts..." Late-night parties, boyfriends, short hair and knees wide apart were all withheld in my Manila, but I found compensation in a lifelong friend: books. Books bought, borrowed, books outside the classroom, books read by the light of a torch under the blanket. It was a time when I absorbed everything like a sponge; from library books to lectures on Greek and Latin epics to whispered rumors filling the air as the country headed toward martial law. Within the sanctified premises of Assumption Convent, I got a glimpse of how the uppermost class lives. At the same time, I got a whiff of the politics that thrives in the unlikeliest places—some of the young nuns, Christian radicals, would go on to become courageous opponents of the Marcos regime.

From Manila, across the Pacific, then from west coast to east. My address was getting crowded, but no one, young lady or otherwise, can be untouched by living in New York. In this city nationality did not seem to matter, especially if you were twenty-three years old, and had your first apartment, your first job, and your first taste of complete independence. There were books and art and music and films in New York. And there was more. Everything about the city was a challenge, whether it was the smelly subways at two in the morning; crazy, murderous Son of Sam on the loose (he was partial to women with long hair); or the aggressive squirrels in Central Park who waited to grab lunch from anyone who let down their guard. Most of all, living in New York was learning to be alone and enjoying it; learning to be a survivor.

Then there was Madras (or there was; now there's Chennai). I discovered that my Palghat Tamil was a source of much hilarity for the "real Tamils"; I would have to relearn my mother tongue. But there was compensation. Where else but in Madras would the neighbors leave a tray full of fresh, hot food at your doorstep because you have been working all day and now have a two-hour music lesson? (I assumed the food was sent in appreciation of my singing, not to keep my mouth full and quiet.) Madras during the day was Mount Road, where I worked and had post-lunch tea and conversation at Spencer's Fiesta café. Sometimes, during a long power cut, I would take my books and papers and settle down to work in the swanky Connemara Hotel Ladies' Room.

All the pleasures of Madras seemed simple and wholesome. Sitting on the sands in Marina Beach or the quieter Eliot Beach once the sea breeze had "set in" every evening. Closing down the kitchen once the music season began in December, because the music *sabhas* rivaled each other in cooking tempting accompaniments to their concerts.

But partaking of all such sweetness and light usually meant following the rules. It was in Madras that I discovered I was an anomalous creature: a single woman. I was determined to live within walking distance of the Music Academy. But this was Mylapore, the heart of brahmin country, and it took me months to find a place to rent. Landlords and landladies interviewed me and invariably found me wanting. If I didn't have a husband, where was my father, or at least my brother? One landlord in Luz raised my hopes by agreeing to rent his flat to me as long as I didn't cook eggs. Just when I thought we had a deal, he came up with one more condition: under no circumstance would I be dropped home by a man on a motorcycle. I wish I had asked him if he felt more kindly toward cars.

Once I had found a flat in a hospitable compound in Alwarpet, I also learned how to juggle the contradictory claims of different worlds in the same city. My Madras had *kacheris* of inspiring music, music that moved me though I did not believe in the words that were sung. But my Madras also had reading groups and public meetings and women's organizations and rallies, all challenging the complacent rigidities of the city I had grown to love. To reject, or even criticize convention, parts of your heritage, it helps to be on intimate terms with it. You have to have stakes, pretty high stakes, in the world you want to change, or dissect and write about. Madras showed me, almost painlessly, what my stakes were all about; as Indian, as modern Indian, as modern Indian woman, as modern Indian woman writer...

Bangalore was, on the face of it, less intense. It was Time Out. There were long walks in Lal Bagh. Or sometimes, an eight-minute walk before I discovered that not only was I hungry, but also practically at the doors of MTR (Mavalli Tiffin Rooms, shades of R.K. Narayan). And everyone else in Lal Bagh was headed to MTR for their daily fix of *masal dosai* with homemade butter.

There was a man in MTR, a dark, skinny man with a long face and an even longer, doleful coat. Diamond studs glittered in his earlobes. I thought of him as the soul of MTR, and a distant relation of my Assumption Convent nuns. His solemn face silently assured me that whatever change came to the world, good or bad, there was always a prim corner in Bangalore that would remain untouched, a museum frozen in time. As he led each hungry customer to a hard and narrow bench to partake of the MTR ritual, he would slip a booklet like a benediction into our hands. The booklet began: "Please remember: Cleanliness is next to Godliness." It went on to make appeals to MTR patrons:

"Please avoid combing of hair anywhere in the premises, as the fallen hairs are likely to blow over to the dishes, served. Please refrain from leaning back on chairs and also touching the wall to avoid soiling."

But in gentle Bangalore it was possible to remember that there is beauty in the world, even in a city, even in a city without the sea. Little Lal Baghs sprang up here and there to civilize the place. There were trees and flowers and bushes, there were illogically meandering houses with gardens. And in many such houses, shaded by jacaranda, gulmohar, laburnum, and obscenely fecund jackfruit, there were women's tales, the sort old women surround you with when you hear their advice and dreams and secrets. They were, in turn, exasperating, funny, fascinating. Pregnancy and motherhood take you to parts of the city you have not seen before.

Finally, the more or less current address, Delhi. Delhi flaunts staid power, completely different from the glamorous brazenness of Bombay and New York. Perhaps this is why its population of transients, who have been in the city fifteen, twenty years, still think they are from some other city or on their way to another. I, too, thought of myself as a transient for the first few months. This was not hard to do because my Hindi, which I thought fluent, turned out to be a mongrel called Bambaiyya. I had trouble with the gender demands of *shudh* Hindi, as well as the idea of purity prefixed to the language I was expected to speak.

Then I was caught in the open by a Delhi *aandhi*. It was perfect, the drama of dust swirling round the boastful Qutb Minar and the cautionary ruins of Tughlakhabad. Delhi can infect even a mere writer with the grandiose scale—be they ambitions of conquest or sagas of retribution. I still do not think of myself as a loyal or monogamous *dilliwalli*. Till I moved to Bangalore, and then Delhi, I had always lived by the sea or close to it. But it was in these two cities that I learned to love and live, to bear books and children, despite my ache for the sea. Sometimes I think my long apprenticeship came to an end and I became a writer because I moved to a landlocked city. And till I became a writer, I thought I had only one city at a time: the one that was my home then. It's when I began writing that I realized the people I imagined wanted to live in Anycity, both smaller and bigger than the cities I had lived in. This Anycity, my writer's anycity, is landlocked. But the sea is never far away. Its insistent call is the stuff of memory, dream and imagination.

So Anycity looks at the sea—the one near it or the one imagined into existence—because always, even if you live there, there has to be a way out of the place, a view of other places. Anycity has a Qutb Minar. Not having an ambitious, foolishly boastful tower or two would be like living in a city without men. Anycity has rocky lovers' haunts like Delhi's Parthasarathy Plateau and free concerts on the sands as in Chennai's Eliot's Beach, and rich libraries overflowing with books. English is tolerated, but only if there is a happy (and impure) Babel of languages in the background. As for the people: there is such a variety, such motley crowds of shapes and features and colors, that there are a thousand disagreements, passion (public and private), even occasional consensus. There is *bhelpuri* sold on the road, the kind you can mix yourself. There are no vigilance squads or *senas* or *senes* or *dals* or *parishads* or Talibans to tell you what to think or how to think it.

Having lived in more than one city, having lost my heart several times over, I now switch on my laptop, or if there is a power cut, pick up a pen, and find myself in Anycity. The kind of city with many histories, stories within a story that begins, enticingly, "Once there was a city..."

Once there was; or once I saw, I loved. And later? Now? Cities don't stand still, even for old flames. When you meet a city again, there is an awkward reunion. You have to relearn its body, see it with two competing eyes, past and present.

MANILA 1974: THE SARI AND THE FAN

In the early months of 2005, a burglar broke into the small flat in Delhi I then used as a workplace. I didn't chase the police about following up my complaint. Instead I wasted time speculating on what the burglar made of the place. (I don't know that it was only one man, but that seemed neater for purposes of speculation.) I imagined his disappointment at the rows and rows of books, not dusted as often as they should be. Perhaps he noticed, with disgust, how many unfinished manuscripts sat forlorn on the tables and in the cabinets. At any rate, he only trashed some of them.

When this man found the flat's one "Godrej" cupboard—an imitation one called "Be Happy"—his faith in happiness must have been restored. (There were large patches of blood-colored *gutka* spit on the floor by the cupboard, patches I took as evidence of relief.) Of course, there was no cash or jewelry in the Godrej, so his night was wasted. But he got a consolation prize—my three wedding saris that I had stored in the cupboard, just in case my offspring decided to marry in a more suitable fashion than I did. He also got a bonus—the fourth silk sari, a sari M.S. Subbulakshmi gave me when I was nineteen years old. I had never found occasion to wear the sari; it had too much gold for that. But in December 2004, when M.S. died, I took it out, admired it, and promised myself I would wear it one day.

No one in her right mind would associate Subbulakshmi with Imelda Marcos. One was a great singer, much loved by those who knew her or those who had heard her voice raised in song. The other was the Iron Butterfly—a dictator's hard, ambitious wife, given to wearing *ternos* with exaggerated butterfly sleeves and owning a shocking number of shoes. But I met both women in the same year. More accurately, I met Imelda Marcos briefly, in a group, because of Subbulakshmi's visit to Manila. The pineapple fiber fan I got as a token of my visit to Malacañang Palace lay among the mementoes of the years in the same cupboard. The burglar took Subbulakshmi's sari and threw Imelda's highly wrought fan on the floor.

There is some moral here, I suspect. The fan, which I had pretty much forgotten, now serves to make me remember and mourn Subbulakshmi all over again.

* * *

In 1974, I was at that awful point suffered by so many young people, between my B.A. and M.A., unsure of what to do with myself. I spent most of this restless year with my parents, who then lived in Manila. The high point of this limbo-like year was M.S. Subbulakshmi's visit to Manila to receive the Ramon Magsaysay award.

Soon after the award was announced, we also heard that Subbulakshmi was to be our houseguest, along with her husband Sadasivam and his daughter Radha. The closest we came to having family heroes and heroines were Carnatic musicians. But still, I was surprised to see my mother's shining eyes and barely suppressed excitement. My mother is the sort who is, in principle, scornful of celebrity worship. If we admired anyone only for fame or social position, she liked to ask, with great sarcasm, "Has her head grown a horn?" (This is a far more effective question in Tamil.) So my mother's anticipation was a measure of the honor of playing hostess to Subbulakshmi. It was as if she was letting me know that anyone with eyes to see and ears to hear would understand that Subbulakshmi was not just an accomplished musician.

I saw my mother's point the instant I set eyes on Subbulakshmi. I had grown up hearing her music; I had seen any number of photographs in newspapers and magazines. Still, her beauty, the quality of her beauty, came as a discovery. The innocent eyes and the warm smile; the fragrance of jasmine and sandalwood about her; and the soft-spoken voice that never seemed to say anything unkind even if someone was asking for a put-down: all these came together wonderfully in Subbulakshmi. Part of her beauty was her genuine lack of consciousness of the fuss and attention surrounding her. Once or twice, sitting next to her, I heard her humming under her breath as people made the kind of long and fulsome speech that accompanies any award. For me, this was the first inkling of how a real artist sets her priorities.

It was after the award ceremony, I think, that Subbulakshmi and her troupe were invited to meet Imelda at a lunch in Malacañang Palace. My mother and I went along. The lunch—the food, that is—was a fiasco. Clearly the Palace officials had not done their homework, and course after course of meat and fish came and went, untouched by the vegetarian guests of honor. Imelda, wearing a dress with her trademark butterfly sleeves, ignored this like a well-trained memsahib. She turned to her neighbor, the Indian ambassador, and asked whether Subbulakshmi was from the North or the South. She then looked soulfully at Subbulakshmi and made a little speech about how she had always found the music of South India especially spiritual. On Imelda's request, Subbulakshmi sang a bhajan at the table, though she must have been tired and hungry, and though there was no accompaniment.

On the way back, Subbulakshmi, incapable of thinking badly of anyone, made only one remark about the visit. Imelda, she said, seemed to have *gnanam*—knowledge, sensibility. Imelda Marcos and gnanam—my mother and I were silent, but we exchanged an eloquent look. We had our revenge, though. When we were back home and Imelda's guests were breaking their fast with *idlis* and curd-rice, Subbulakshmi's daughter opened the extravagantly packed boxes she and her mother had received from Imelda. The boxes were full of cigars.

There was no more talk of Imelda, her gnanam or anything else. Luckily, as a fringe member of the group, I got a fan, not cigars. And for some reason, it still lies in my cupboard all these years later, ready to tell me of the astonishing difference that separates two famous women.

I'd rather have kept the sari as a memento of my meeting with Subbulakshmi. But the burglar changed that story. The sari and the story would remain mine only if I imagined a suitable end to the burglar's encounter with my cupboard. I resisted the unhelpful suggestions of friends that my silk saris were melted down to yield a few tiny lumps of silver. This is what I saw, though I had not seen my burglar: there was a woman in his life, and he had given her Subbulakshmi's green and gold sari. The sari, despite its years of hiding, despite its being stolen, had brought grace—some kind of soul-changing music—into this woman's life.

But this gentle mood of reconciliation came to me later. By then the aging century had faded and given way to the new millennium. To cities where the old homes of the seventies sat waiting in memory, a little too far from the twenty-first century.

NEW YORK 2004: A REALLY GOOD GOODBAR

I left New York in April 1978. It took me weeks to say goodbye. I walked its streets, memorizing the city block by block. Perhaps I didn't do a good job. Perhaps the unconscious does strange things with precious memories. For months after I returned to Bombay, I had dreams of New York, but all the dreams were nightmares. These nightmares reduced my years in New York to late-night commutes in the subway, fearful of an encounter with the Son of Sam; and the one time someone tried to get past the double locks of my door.

Everyone who has lived in New York has at least one scary experience to recount. It's almost an initiation ritual. Till you have got past that, you are little more than a tourist. I had spent many a lunch hour at work casually discussing survival tactics on confronting intruders—crazy men, cockroaches and water bugs in that order. When it finally happened, I spoke into the "hear" part of the contraption on the wall that allowed residents to communicate with the building doorman. I tried desperately to hear him on the "speak" part of the machine. It worked, however; whoever it was, left. I never found out whether the person had malicious intent. When I opened the door a crack an hour later, one or two other doors on the floor opened as well. Along with my unknown neighbors (one of whom was rumored to be from the Mob) I peeked into the sad yellow-tinged corridor that smelled of stale air. There was no one, but all of us shut our doors quickly.

* * *

I didn't think I would ever go back to New York, or to those years of youthful discovery. I did return, but they were brief work-filled visits. I was visiting America, not New York. Then, in 2004, I spent an extra week in the city, just to look around and meet old friends. Invariably the subject came around to a different sort of intruder who wanted to change the New Yorker's notion of home forever. When I lived in Manhattan all those years ago, it used to be *Where were you when the lights went out?* That had seemed ominous enough in those days of innocence. Now the inescapable question was *Where were you when the Towers came down?* The next question, *Are your friends and family all right?* was difficult to ask, and surely even more difficult to answer.

I decided to take a day off from this new New York and travel to the past. Was it really twenty-six years since I had seen 253, 72nd St between Broadway and Riverside Drive in the late-afternoon light? Had I imagined the place I lived in?

Getting out of the subway, I knew the past was past. The triangular little park outside the subway station, a park we residents spoke of boastfully as our own Needle Park, was now almost pretty. I looked at it in wonder and walked down the street, ready to see a hole where 253 used to be.

The building had not been torn down; 253 was still there. It was still uglier than the buildings on either side. There was still no 13th floor, so my dark studio apartment—was it 14G? 14H?—must be sitting up there. Youth and innocence were not figments of memory. As I stood in the foyer, a suspicious lump taking shape in my throat, I saw an old woman get into the elevator. She reminded me of another old woman with a walker whom I had tried to help into this elevator many years back. That woman had spat at me viciously, "Don't touch me!" I held back now, wiser with the years. Then a child ran into the foyer, headed for the elevator, and helped the old woman. A child returning from school! I couldn't recall seeing children, regular families, in the building before. Maybe I had just not noticed them?

The street outside had also become wholesome—sanitized, I thought with some bitterness, forgetting the dirt and fears and spitting old women for a moment. I saw two yoga centers. The Gristede's next door had given way to a pharmacy. I remembered an urban legend: when an establishment moves in New York, the rats and cockroaches have to decide whether they, too, will leave, or stay back and take a chance with the new occupants. I wondered what the vermin of Gristede's decided. Maybe they didn't have a choice; maybe they were exterminated as the street let itself be cleaned up.

The ninety-nine-cent cinema where I saw all my first Bergman and Truffaut and Buñuel was gone; so was the charming café called copper something or the other. There were more shops; barbecue and grill places, homey and inviting. I crossed the street, and went into the bar which some in the neighborhood liked to believe was the model for Goodbar. It was now a respectable Empire State café. There was graffiti on the tables, but there was a chic quality to the graffiti. An impatient young waiter advised me to add my name to the table and forget the past.

I wanted to take his advice. I also wanted to believe the old friend who told me that now more than ever, despite 9/11, despite the war on terror, New York could never be just America. It will always be an island off the mainland of America.

From America to India—cities get cleaned up with the years, beautified so they hide their memories. They replace old terrors with new ones, secretive old fantasies with the trendy kind that can be flaunted.

BANGALORE 2008:
NAMING GLOBAL FANTASIES IN BENGALURU

Just the year before, Bangalore had officially become Bengaluru. So my escape from Delhi in sunstruck June was not to the Bangalore I knew, name-wise, and, I discovered, otherwise.

I was in a small roadside stationery shop in the new Bangalore, stocking up on pens, pencils, and notebooks. I found the bill surprisingly steep. When I asked the shopkeeper why ordinary ballpoint pens were so expensive, I got a sharp reply from him. Maybe he could sense some of the baggage those who live in the capital carry with them to other parts of India. Maybe he wanted to let me know I was a notebook-buying dinosaur who didn't know how much the times have changed. He looked at me scornfully and boasted, "This is not Delhi. This is Bengaluru. Naturally the prices are higher."

Over the next week, I discovered some other little ways in which old friends of Bengaluru could now be, in a manner of speaking, Bangalored.

To begin with, certain words had become essential to any conversation. No one took a lowly bus to Mysore anymore; they took a Volvo. (I heard you could also take a Volvo to the new privatized airport, which involved something of a journey from the city.) Young and upwardly mobile families no longer went out on Sundays; they either de-stressed or bonded. The stress-conscious could look up weekend getaways on websites like getoffurass.com. Middle-level management could bond with spouse and children at "spa resorts." In the spa resort I visited one Sunday, the hearty voice of the master of ceremonies had a desperate edge to it. He was urging fathers (who were drinking beer) and mothers (who were shy) to join their children in dancing to *kajra re*. I suspected such a Sunday was punishment for overusing and misusing two words that used to be respectable: concept and issues. If almost anything is a concept, you are bound to have issues that call for either a getaway, or bonding with the family, instead of taking a weekend nap.

The new devotion to the word "issues" was a special case. I had to admit it had been a while since I heard, in any of the Indian metros, a question such as "So you've been married five years. How many issues?" Instead I had been hearing of X's ego issues, Y's alcohol issues and Z's adjustment issues. But in Brave New Bengaluru, I found it's possible to have pure, unadulterated issues. If I asked the man taking apart my computer what was wrong with it, he said, with suitable gravitas, "It has issues." If someone meeting me for coffee was late, he would text me that he had issues, would I please wait longer. I looked round hopefully for a hoarding advertising issueless mobiles, or a building called Issueless Manor, and was disappointed to find no one had got there yet.

I did find residence-names which had no issues with letting everyone know where you are most at home. There was the somewhat dated regal genre, the Belvedere Mansions and Barton Courts and Residency Manors that sounded like they belonged in an old-fashioned "residential colony," not the more up-to-date complex or township, or the cutting-edge integrated enclave that boasts three theme gardens. There was the evergreen nature-gone-purple sort of address: Cascading Meadows, Canary Wharf, Rainbow Drive, and even, in a stroke of anthropomorphic magic, Laughing Waters. There was the somewhat cryptic Sobha Fiorella, possibly an indication of how at home the residents are with pizza and pasta; or Aquila Heights, where the residents are, perhaps, more partial to tequila than Mr. Mallya's beer. There was the more plain-speaking Sobha Lifestyle and Ferns Icon, or the evolved Brigade Harmony.

Going by what it calls its homes, the new IT-ed and MNC-ed Bengaluru reassured me that I wouldn't have to take that Volvo to the airport too often. It was possible to stay in the global section of the city and see the Riviera or Palm Springs. It was possible for fusion lovers to declare their mixed allegiance by buying or renting in Mantri España, Purva Venezia, or Sterling Shalom.

People in such globalized homes can hardly be expected to shop in places with ordinary names. The little neighborhood shops that aspire the hardest seemed to prefer two names, like a main title and a subtitle. A garment store, for instance, invited me to *Come Fall in Love*; the subtitle, for mystified outsiders, was *Western Wear for Women*. Next door, the hole-in-the-wall selling underclothes had an even better subtitle: *the Complete Underscene Solution*.

The words that are bandied about in our daily conversation say something about us. Our words and our names—the names we make up and attach to our given names like a postal address—say a lot about the new fantasies we want to live out.

Perhaps a friend's account of a family ceremony—appropriately for our purposes, a naming ceremony for a visiting Non-Resident Indian baby—illustrates this best. The baby's grandmother was the family repository of tradition. Having just returned from America, she waxed magisterial to stay-at-homes about how easy it is to observe *madi*—the requirements of purity and pollution—in American homes, because there were no servants, and the basements could be kept free of outsiders. Once the naming was done, the grandmother took the baby onto her lap and cooed at him. But she didn't use his new name. She crooned, "*Puttani* green-card holder! Littlest American citizen!"

The ideal fusion fantasy is a global address that allows you to hold on to the safe familiarity of provincialism. I don't know if the baby gurgled in grateful response, but I hope he did.

The old Bangalore, and the Bengaluru before that, the unlikely ancestor of the present one, were still there, though their oxygen level has been dipping day by day. Garden City is mostly gone with the uprooting of venerable trees, and so is the Pensioner's Paradise. Now it's not just Electronics City and India's Silicon Valley, but also "one of the most happening cities in India where you can find all the high-tech trends of developed societies."

With the first rains in Delhi, I got back, feeling put in my place. I lived then on a campus where the areas have names like Uttarakhand and Dakshinapuram, and the hostels Brahmaputra and Tapti. After Bengaluru, the Delhi campus seemed woefully unaware of the globally acceptable. Its place names only told of being somewhere in India, and that didn't seem enough anymore.

My newfound humility didn't last, though. There was no changing the stubborn self-confidence of the university. But I happened to go to the suburbs, what is now called NCR, the National Capital Region. Gurgaon—or Gergen, as an English acquaintance pronounces it—showed me a worthy North Indian rival to Bengaluru. Driving past malls and condominiums with names like Hamilton Court and Celebrity Homes, and a building with cement awnings like the skirts of maternity swimsuits, I found it. I found the ideal global address, an exercise in naming fantasies that would have done the NRI grandmother in Bengaluru proud. *Manhattan Personal Floors.* I felt a flash of triumph. The waters may laugh in Bangalore; but it takes the wild suburbia of Gergen to make Manhattan, or at least one floor of it, an Indian's personal property.

It is hard, though, to make Gergen a reliable teacher. It took Mumbai to teach me that personal property is serious business; so serious that a whole city, with its weight of memories, homes, and once-upon-a-time homes, can become real estate sold by the square inch.

MUMBAI 2008, 2009, 2011: PHOENIX DYING, PHOENIX RISING

In mid-2008, I spent a couple of weeks setting up house for my son, who had just moved to Mumbai to take up his first job. I arrived there full of confidence. After all, Bombay was my first home. As for Wadala, where he had found a flat, the place was next door to Matunga, scene of my Bombay Tamil childhood. I was full of plans; I had lists in my bag. I looked down at Bombay as the plane began its descent, almost expecting the city to wave its cap at me for old times' sake. What I saw instead was a spreading patch of melanoma-like slums. Bombay-Mumbai, once it became *the* Indian city of success, has always had slums. Slum lords have always reigned supreme in this city. But were the slums always so large? Or had they grown inescapable to my eyes because I no longer lived there, passing by them every day?

Once I was in the flat in Wadala, on the seventeenth floor of a building that looked out at its four companion high-rises, I was in yet another city. My Bombay was a place where you stood in the balcony. Even if you were forced by greed or necessity or folly to enclose the balcony, there was always enough to see from the windows. The city has trained generations of voyeurs. I could recall long pre-television evenings standing in the balcony that overlooked the road, never short of scenes and people to look at. All the action and poignant detail of human drama would play out before me, on a very wide screen.

But this building, so smart, so glossy—with a swimming pool downstairs and security guards to keep the nosy city away—had only a caged ledge, not a balcony. I climbed onto this ledge, bent so I could fit in there, and peered at the view outside. If I risked a crick in the neck, I could see a suggestive glimmer of water in the distance. The height of the flat and the huddled-for-safety buildings made it hard to see the slums below. But this is a tenacious city, its people not easily silenced. I found the alarm clock could easily be replaced every morning with the shrill non-angelic voices of children singing in the school morning assembly. Evenings provided an aural metaphor of India's unity in diversity. The local mosque's call to prayer pierced the air all the way up to the seventeenth floor. Hymn-like sounds wafted up at intermittent intervals, to remind me that I was in Wadala Parish with its headquarters in nearby Antop Hill. And late into the night, as if to confirm that this was a Mumbai ruled by parties partial to Hindus, bhajan after off-key bhajan triumphantly rose up the air to challenge my aging memory of Wadala.

I was nine years old when my parents found a Carnatic music teacher in Wadala, willing to teach children. Between 1963 and 1965, my sister and I commuted sleepily every Sunday morning for our weekly music lesson. We went by bus or car from Nepean Sea Road (big city) to Wadala (small town). To us, Wadala seemed a hick town with a few stray buildings, a general grimy wilderness, petrol depots, and oil refineries in nearby Sewri. The only people we knew in Wadala were South Indians.

The view from the lone bedroom window in the high-rise flat now showed me that I could remedy this immediately. All I had to do was go downstairs, join the purposeful army of ant-sized people moving at fixed hours from road to train station, train station to road.

Instead I turned away from the window and went back to my task of raiding the new batch of cockroaches that would have crept into the kitchen via the air-conditioning ducts. I felt a frisson of spite; the slum lords, real estate touts and "developers" could overrun Mumbai with posh towers, each box in these towers worth crores. But the subterranean universe would survive—the mice and cockroaches and ants under the gloss. They would serve as ugly and necessary reminders of the people and lives far below.

* * *

Just as people work hard at closing their eyes to what they don't want to see, they also train memories to wither. Places, too, become new places as if nothing was there before.

A year later, during a visit to the city in 2009, my son and I went to a film at one of the multiplex theaters in Lower Parel. I had not seen Parel for years—when I saw it last it was still the mill area, backbone of the textile industry. This new Parel was glamorous, but I could not shake off the suspicion that it was delusional. I could see this mall-ed Parel—all five-star glass and air conditioning, all multiplex and corporate park and hotel and residential tower—only on half of a split screen that let me see images of an earlier time. Without these unglamorous images, Mumbai's Lower Parel, hip, cool, expensive, and happening, would be a childish dream. It would have no soul, no sense of history or human endeavor. Could a place suffer from amnesia in its sights and sounds and smells? Could High Street Phoenix sit around me, making believe it was Hong Kong or Shanghai when it was really Phoenix Mills?

I sensed a collective memory here under the noise and glitter of Maximum Mumbai Shining. I saw myself on a Bombay street in 1979, listening rapt to an indomitable little woman standing on a lorry. Her name was Ahilya Rangnekar. She and her fellow activists set up the Parel Mahila Sangh in the forties, an organization that brought together, through its working class membership, pressing issues of class and gender. I wondered what Ahilyabai, or the textile workers she led, would make of the plush stores in the new Parel, the prices so many people seemed to be able to pay without hesitation. Maybe they would take heart from the fact that the smokeless chimney stands disapprovingly in the midst of High Street Phoenix, like an all-seeing sentinel.

But between the comrades' Parel and this Parel with a smokeless chimney, a link in the memory chain intrudes. In December 1967, the headquarters of the Communist Party of India in Parel, in the heart of the textile area, was attacked by the hoodlums of the growing "army" of the city—the Shiv Sena. In June 1970, a leader of the textile workers and member of the legislative assembly was assassinated. The Sena and its own management-friendly unions dealt a body blow to the workers' movements, helping change Parel over the years from a scene of political ideas and action to high-value real estate.

Bombay, ever willing to stretch its islands to accommodate newcomers in search of a living, began to change. Anyone in the crowd could become an outsider any day—South Indians, North Indians, Muslims. The crowds persisted; but the crowd, the "masses," have, over the years, been beaten by the mob. In places like Parel, they no longer waved red flags and sang songs extolling strength and unity. Instead they exhibit strength in numbers by running extortion rackets, vandalizing shops selling Valentine's Day cards, or trashing theaters screening films "against Indian culture."

A phoenix was born, it was fed and fattened, even as another lay in its death throes.

* * *

Numbers are always deceptive in cities like Mumbai. The reborn phoenix had drawn a crowd, but the real crowd, the human sea, flowed where it always had outside and into the Victoria Terminus. On my way to Colaba, my youthful haunt where my son had moved in 2009, I stopped by VT. I used to take trains here, mostly the intercity trains to the South.

Like its host city, VT has changed its name; it became CST—Chhatrapati Shivaji Terminus—in 1996. I stood there, hating the new name. But at least from the outside, the place had not changed. It has the same spectacular gothic façade, the same sea of humanity. I was the only person not moving. Now that I was an outsider, I could stand there like a gawking tourist, letting the building and the ever-moving crowds compete for my attention. The people won. I remembered a silly game a friend and I would play outside VT when we were happy twenty-year-olds. Our theory was that you didn't have to make an effort to walk outside VT. If you stood in the belly of the crowd, you would be moved by a human conveyor belt; all you needed to do was know which way you wanted to go.

I forgot about games when I went in now. Commuters rushed to trains or waited, their minds elsewhere already. Or maybe a few were remembering what happened here in November 2008.

That old woman standing so still, as if waiting for life and the city to do their worst. Or that long-faced child, a streaky black mark on his face to keep the evil eye away, staring vacantly ahead. Maybe even the gainfully employed ones, those laughing as they talked on their cell phones, would remember once the phone call was over. How could they forget? Two young men in innocuous T-shirts walking into familiar old VT one ordinary night, AK-47s in hand, opening fire in the passenger hall! Nothing could have prepared VT regulars for such a thing. Had a new fear added its weight to all the pinpricks of everyday life in Mumbai? That young woman in a cotton sari holding her bag close to her and frowning at her watch—was she afraid that the train would not take her home to her children some evening?

* * *

I made my way from VT to Colaba, pausing to acknowledge the art deco Regal Cinema which gave me the treats of my childhood, from *The Sound of Music* and Laurel and Hardy to my first ice-cream cone. I was staying in a building right on the Causeway, the third-floor balcony (not enclosed), practically in the middle of the Causeway. It certainly felt like it once the traffic began at about seven in the morning. I would get up as early as I could and walk down the Causeway while it looked like an aging star before she had put on her makeup. At this hour, Colaba still belonged to its long-ago owners, the koli fisherfolk. I watched as a large group of fisherwomen, short saris tied tight round their thighs like pantaloons, balanced overflowing baskets on their heads and yelled to each other across the street. They were just as tough and loud and stunning as I remembered them from thirty, forty years back.

Once the fisherwomen were gone, the cats emerged. This part of Colaba, close to Sassoon Docks, must be cat heaven. Even the pavement was encrusted with refuse which had a crustacean look to it. When they were not feeding, many of these cats retired to their heights—the ledges of buildings, lower roofs. I watched one such cat from the kitchen window; it had claimed squatter rights on the roof of the petrol pump below. I remembered with a shock: this must be the petrol pump the terrorists threatened to blow up in 2008. Which meant that the five-story building down the lane, the one draped with green cloth, must be Nariman House turned Chabad House, another awful stop for the terrorists. In all my years in Bombay, I had never seen this building before. Looking at it now, I felt I knew it well despite the green curtain. I, like the rest of India, had watched the commandos landing on its rooftop on television.

* * *

In 2011, I returned to the Colaba area, but this time I stayed in a boutique hotel in Apollo Bunder called Gordon House. The hotel, small in size but large in ambition, had a selection of Mediterranean, Scandinavian, and country rooms. The place was barely five minutes away from the Gateway of India, the Taj Hotel sitting across as if waiting to ease the visitor's first day in the country. Apollo Bunder had got cleaned up; as a college student in the seventies I had to walk briskly down these shady lanes ruled by drug pushers, pimps, and touts, and their sleazy customers.

Now I found myself walking twice a day to the Gateway. There is something about an arch, an arch facing the sea, with an impossibly ambitious name like Gateway of India. The Gateway is to an island that is only the tip of a bewildering, beloved place called India. The Gateway is to the sea, the sea which brought other people to these shores; and more important, a sea that allows you to escape India, take a breather from its grasp.

The Gateway was trying to move with the times. There was a barricade set up before the arch; and there were the ubiquitous rifle-toting security men. Otherwise, the Gateway looked just as it used to, a little dour from standing still and silent for so long. The pigeons feeding in the square, feathered old-timers of the city, were as greedy as ever. I leaned against the wall dividing sea and city and considered the Taj. In 2009, I had been told there were bullet marks on some wall in VT, but I hadn't looked for them. Now I could not escape the marks on the wall of the Taj.

Three years had already passed since the Taj acquired its wounds, its scars. The hotel had long been open for business again. The memories of that blood- and fear-soaked November night, the fearful days that followed, had already seeped deep into the sturdy old wall. If the Taj was now wearing a new face, it was not apparent. Maybe it was we who looked at it who wore the new face. I turned away and stared at the sea, old nursemaid of childhood.

The Arabian Sea was a seething opaque gray. The sea, bordered with a dirty barricade of rocks; the city, hemmed in by an inadequate wall between land and rock. A mean voice I didn't recognize whispered in my ear: "This city, your first love, is nothing but a mass of real estate. From childhood homes and mills to Ambani's ridiculous mansion to the slumdogged stretch of Dharavi, it's just yards of real estate that make people push and jostle, cheat and steal and murder." Maybe the sea knew about real estate, considering that the land reclaimed from it was also the most coveted.

The sea must have seen so many come to this place, friends, foes, people in search of a home. It must have seen the city invented over and over again. But the sea of childish fears and joys, the sea that still laps into my middle-aged dreams, said nothing. If it had been friendlier, if it had deigned to speak to me, the sea could have told me that people, names, dreams, and fears come and go. The sea has flowed past and around and alongside it all, Mumba, Bom Baia, Bombay, Mumbai. The sea knows it's home, or almost home. It's never going to let it go.

2

TWO CITIES OF VICTORY

HAMPI 1996, VIJAYANAGAR 1565:
THE MOVING SHALL EVER STAY

Early on a November morning, armed with a water bottle, a notebook, and a pen, I walked down a quiet country road. I was on my way to Hampi, the site of a medieval city. The city was called Vijayanagar, City of Victory, and it was the fabled capital of a great empire in South India.

Vijayanagar was described as a wonder-city by medieval travelers. Firsthand accounts of the city's best years were written by the Persian ambassador, chronicler and Islamic scholar Abdur Razzaq; by the Portuguese envoy Domingo Paes and his compatriot Fernão Nuniz, a horse trader; by the Italian merchant Niccolò dei Conti, and the Russian traveler Athanasius Nikitin. They wrote of the lofty stone-built dwellings of royals, nobles, and merchants interspersed with the squalid habitations of the poor; the elaborately built aqueducts which watered the rich gardens and woods lying side by side with luxurious crops of rice and sugarcane; the wonderfully carved temples of Hindu deities, the renowned brahmin colleges and schools; the colorful festivals, the bazaars heaped with pearls, emeralds, and roses; the community of poets, philosophers, musicians, dancing girls—all the glitter of Hindu medieval court life.

* * *

When I got to Hampi in 1996, I could only see the ruins of what Razzaq and company must have seen. What remains of Vijayanagar is on the southern bank of the Tungabhadra River. But "remains" is a misleading word. The site incorporates a progression from plains, to flat land ringed with hills, to mountains with the river flowing around and between. Spread over twenty-six square kilometers is an array of fortification walls, temple complexes, stables, palaces, baths, and watchtowers.

The ruins were unlike anything I had seen before, and most Indians have seen plenty of ruins. But Hampi, like the Vijayanagar that was, offers only a part of itself to the naked eye. The rest, stories that reconstruct the heaps of broken blocks, the crushed masonry and fragments of sculpture, reside in a place accessible only to the imagination.

The landscape before me was certainly real. It was stark, powerful, as if holding out a challenge. Boulders of odd shapes and sizes balanced precariously on each other, casting deep, sharp-edged shadows. These giants of strange shapes surrounded me. Their powerful bodies pierced the skyline; their faces wore a menacing look.

I felt very alone. The routine world and its mundane demands had vanished from view. I had left behind the twentieth century, and with it, all the comforting scenes of rural Karnataka.

Then the silence was broken by tinkling bells. I started, turned around. A girl with a stick was leading her goats, bells round their necks, to graze in the city of victory. She had on a green blouse with puff sleeves, and a blue skirt a size too big for her. Her long hair was tied with a ribbon, but some strands had escaped and flew wildly about her face. As she passed me, she pointed at a pair of rocks leaning on each other. *Akka-thangi*, she told me: Big Sister and Little Sister. Then the girl and the goats went on, leaving me alone again. Only the landscape seemed just a little different. The boulders were still strangely shaped and positioned; they were still far too big. But they now held, in their protective ring, the ruins that stretched in every direction around me, the walls, temples, and palaces that sprouted out of overgrown grass and peered from behind rocks and bushes. Maybe the girl and her sisters of stone had touched the place with magic. If I looked hard enough, a city may be brought to life.

* * *

The year is 1565. Vijayanagar is at war. But as in the case of many powerful cities, this is not unusual. A visitor to the city would sense no danger or dread. Clearly the city does not expect the battle to touch it and disrupt its daily business. The seaports are busy as ever. Strings of pack bullocks, camels and asses weighed down with merchandise wend their way past the tax collectors at the city gate. A bell in a temple rings; its clear voice echoes up in the hills. Far below, litters are carried out of the *zenana*, guarded by burly eunuchs. Some of the royal women are on their way to the bath or the temple.

The puppet king, Sadasiva, remains in his royal chamber. Perhaps he has learned to enjoy luxury without either power or its responsibilities. (Later, in 1900, a civil servant turned Indologist, Robert Sewell, would write disapprovingly that Sadasiva led a "a profitless life in inglorious seclusion."[1])

The puppet king is at home. The city is at war, but the enemy is an old one and has not succeeded in hurting the city in living memory. Battle is a regular business of a great city; the citizens pursue the other necessary businesses—trade, money, religion and prayers, learning, love and sex, prostitution. Like his fellow citizens, old Rama Raya, king de facto, prefers to affect haughty indifference to the movement of the enemy. (Sewell quotes the Persian historian Firishtah on Rama Raya's treatment of the enemies' ambassadors: "He treated their ambassadors with scornful language, and regarded their enmity as of little moment."[2])

The enemy may be an old one, but this time four of the Deccan sultanates have united to form a confederacy. Besides, security is the paramount business of a thriving city. As a matter of course Rama Raya has sent two of his brothers with armies to the front. Now he, too, is away from the city, at the scene of action.

* * *

It's Tuesday, January 23. The day before, Rama Raya learned that the enemy was marching southward to attack his army. The enemy was within ten miles of Rama Raya's camp. He was surprised but not alarmed. He had already set about taking all possible measures for defense; his brothers and their armies had joined him. There was no question that the allies would turn tail when faced with an empire's military might.

This morning both sides are ready, with all the forces they can summon.

The troops of Vijayanagar go to battle near the villages of Raksasji and Tagdiji. Two thousand mounted Muslim archers let their arrows fly; the lines of heavy guns follow, the swivels in the rear. Gun-carriages fastened together with ropes and chains, and elephants with sword blades on their tusks, wait at intervals. There are a hundred thousand horses; and six hundred thousand men, drafted from the provinces—what we now know as Karnataka, Andhra, Kerala, and Tamilnadu. Some of the common soldiers wear working clothes and are armed with only a spear or dagger. Others in the infantry have oiled their bare bodies so they will not be easily caught.

The allied troops advance with an infantry of three thousand, and a cavalry of fifty thousand. The army of Bijapur includes a large Maratha regiment in its cavalry; empires and armies can't afford to care about the religious persuasion of their soldiers. Mercenaries make up an important part of all battles to keep the powerful safe.

Rama Raya is carried on to the battlefield in a litter, right to the very center. His advisers have warned him that leading a battle from a litter is a dangerous thing. But he is an old man, and does not wish to be mounted for too long. (Sewell quotes Portuguese chronicler Diego de Couto, who claimed Rama Raya was ninety-six at this time but "as brave as a man of thirty.") Besides, Rama Raya tends to think of all enemies as misbehaving children. Children or not, he orders his men to bring him the head of Hussain Nizam, one of the allies who has dared to take on his army. The other two, Adil Shah and Ibrahim, he wants alive so he can imprison them in iron cages for the rest of their lives.

Suddenly an elephant excited and confused by battle charges at the litter of state. The screaming bearers drop their burden. Before Rama Raya can pick himself up and mount a horse, enemy troops swoop down on him. Confusion reigns. Then the Vijayanagar army sees its commander's head held up high, impaled on a long spear. Confusion gives way to panic. The forces break and scatter. The allies pursue them. A hundred thousand men fall as they are pursued across the river, says Sewell, a river now "dyed red with blood."

The news travels to the city. Rumor claims that the princes of the royal house have returned. They will leave soon after, under a convoy of soldiers and a thousand elephants. The beasts are laden, say people, with coins, bundles of gold and diamonds, and a throne.

Nobles, ministers, whoever can fly has fled. The city is quiet; there is nothing to be done but bury the most treasured of valuables, arm the younger men, and wait. The silence breaks now and then: roving bands of tribesmen from the neighboring jungle loot deserted houses and shops. Three days later, the allied armies reach Vijayanagar. Every soldier piles up his own booty—jewels from palaces, temples, merchants; or tents, arms, horses, and slaves. One of the seized diamonds, claims de Couto, is as large as a hen's egg, "a jewel the Raya affixed to his horse's head-dress."

The search for treasure continues with the help of swords, crowbars, and axes. They aim at idols; smoke rises from palaces and houses. Column after column falls. Narasimha, the man-lion fashioned out of a single granite boulder, loses his arms. The goddess Lakshmi, seated on his left thigh, is reduced to a single arm on his back. The "scenes of savage massacre and horrors," says Sewell, "beggar description."

Two years later, reports the Italian merchant traveler Cesare Federici, when Rama Raya's brother tried to repopulate the city, few people could be induced to return; and the kingdom's capital was moved to Penukonda. The stone-built houses in Vijayanagar still stand, reports Federici, but fit only for "tigers and other wild beasts."

* * *

The city remained a scene of desolation and ruin, but four centuries later, I found no sign of wild beasts. Life reasserted itself in Vijayanagar, above all through the common pilgrim. The oldest temple in the ruins, the Virupaksha temple which celebrates the cosmic marriage of Siva to Pampa, predates the Vijayanagar Empire. This is the sole living monument among the ruins, a temple still used for worship. Here heroes of the Hindu pantheon continue to be born, to marry and reign, impervious to time and change. Pilgrims throng the courtyards of this temple, making their simple offerings of prayer and flowers. They may never build cities of victory, these modern pilgrims. It is unlikely they are either poets or philosophers. But the words of the Kannada medieval poet, Basava, may not be strange to them:

53

The rich
will make temples for Siva.
What shall I,
a poor man,
do?

My legs are pillars,
the body the shrine,
the head a cupola
of gold.

Listen, O lord of the meeting rivers,
things standing shall fall,
but the moving ever shall stay.[3]

Poets prefer to speak of temples, not fortresses. The rich and victorious not only make temples; they also make sure of the city's lines of defense. "Lofty and massive stone walls everywhere crossed the valleys, and led up to and mounted the hillsides," writes Niccolò dei Conti of Vijayanagar's security measures. "The outer lines stretched unbroken across the level country for several miles."

In 1996, when I followed in the footsteps of earlier travelers to Hampi, the walls were still there in broken stretches. So were the "basket-boats" Paes saw, carrying people and oxen across the river to the old city of Anegondi; though the boat I watched, turning round and round, ferried a Frenchwoman with a camera and an Indian on a moped. The boulders remained a part of the city, as did the aqueducts and temples, though many of these were empty, their only devotees bats. In every building I saw block after block of carved lions, warriors, and naked dancing girls. Visiting a tall structure in the zenana, I was told it was a watchtower; later I heard it could be a "pleasure look-out," a viewing tower for the royal women.

Vijayanagar was still being revealed, but modern Hampi competed for my attention.

I had found myself a hotel a short walk from the ruins. The hotel was busy—in addition to Indian and foreign tourists, there was a French film unit in Hampi to make an "action" film. Like all film units, there was an inescapable glamor about these people, and their table was lively. The waiters preferred waiting on them despite the language problem; and though we did not recognize their actors, the rest of us gazed at them like well-trained film-worshiping Indians. The waiter who finally made his way to my table confided that the French film was also to star a monkey; he had heard there may be a kissing scene involving the monkey. Sadly, the monkey was not with its love interest in the restaurant. The waiter then suggested I order Gobi Manchurian, one of the hotel specialties. "Everyone loves our Chinese food, even the French," he assured me. I was not sure what the French made of the hotel's experiments with Chinese food, but I found that the plate of Gobi Manchurian I ate had little to do with either cauliflowers or Manchuria. But there was compensation. This was a place where I could communicate in four languages—English, Tamil, Kannada, and Hindi—and though this well-stocked armory of words did not get me anything more edible than buttered toast, it made me feel confident as I set out for the ruins.

I decided to ignore the busy "living" monuments the tourists seemed partial to and went off to explore on my own. I reached an open space, what may have once been a bazaar. The sun was sharp; I was sweating in my woman-traveling-alone modest outfit. I looked at a young white woman ahead; she was wearing shorts and a tiny halter top. Then two men appeared out of nowhere and raced up to her. They seemed to be selling her something or offering their services as guides. Clearly the transaction did not work. She walked ahead; they screamed "*Sule! Sule!*" at her bare legs and back. The girl must have assumed they were still advertising their wares, and walked on without fear. I cringed. *Sule* in Kannada means whore, and it was difficult for me to pretend I didn't know what they were shouting. But the men looked at me blandly and said in English, "This is old historical sule bazaar. Do you need a guide, auntie?"

By noon, I was far away from brave white girls and aspiring guides. The sun, the ruins, my notebook and water bottle, the crunching sound my shoes made on the ground: there was nothing else. I went into a cavelike enclosure and found an impressive Vishnu reclining there. The place was cool, only it smelled of bats. Any number of people must have seen the Vishnu before, but it was easy to believe I was making a discovery.

But as I walked on, I found the place, the structures, the rocks, too big for me. Maybe I didn't have what it takes to make an explorer? The rocks I passed had warnings painted on them. *No littering. Don't make nuisance. Beware of pickpockets.*

And several beginning *Ladies alone…* I decided to find myself some transport and a companion. I found one easily, an auto driver called Suban, a namesake of one of the Deccan sultans. And he solved my Gobi Manchurian problem; he got me hot light idlis wrapped in banana leaf. We ate together then set out.

Suban looked at the Narasimha statue with me. On an impulse, I asked him, "Do you know the story?" He shook his head, and so began our day of stories, a story, sometimes two, for every figure we stopped at. I noticed Suban liked the stories of unbeatable strength best. Of Narasimha, half man, half lion; of Yali, a mythical tiger, elephant, and horse rolled into one. It didn't take him long to confide the reason for this preference. "You have to be strong to have a son," he informed me. "I have daughters." Considering the number of *lingas* we passed on the rocky surfaces, the ground beneath our feet sprouting a phallus anywhere, I thought it best to stick to the safer stories. Happily, we came upon a four-armed Ganesha at this point. I could only hope the story of an elephant-headed son whose relationship with his parents was somewhat unusual would introduce a healthy note of confusion in Suban's head.

* * *

One evening, Suban and I went up a hill overlooking the river and Krishna Deva's Vittala temple. Suban's auto groaned its way up and came to a halt with a great splutter. We climbed the rest of the way, then sat on the warm hard rocks. Suban was worried about the punishment his auto had just taken; he still had to pay half the loan he had taken to buy it. And he had three daughters, he said, between the ages of two and four. He then pointed out a cluster of tiny stone gateways. Couples who want to conceive, he said, set up two vertical stones and a third on top like a roof. When the child is born, they return to remove the roof, leaving a miniature ruin. We fell silent, the spread of much bigger ruins before us. As the sun went down, the boulders and *gopurams* assumed the faces of brooding strangers.

Looking at the awe-inspiring always seems to bring people closer together. The silence was too good to last. Suban said to me softly, "They shouldn't have broken it down." He looked stricken, as if I had accused him of sacking the city of victory. I knew "they" meant Muslims, but I didn't want to believe it. I didn't want the two of us to be friendly people from two different sides. But my lecture on sides, on shifting sides, was a failure. I knew this even as I gave it to Suban. We went down to the auto in silence. He did not turn up the next morning.

The next day the ruins did not speak to me in the same clear voice. Every time I paused at another grand figure of stone, I found myself thinking of Suban; of my failure to tell him more than the usual stories of godlike creatures.

I could have told him, for instance: there were two petty chieftains in what is now Hampi. Harihara and Bukka were taken to Delhi as prisoners of Muhammed bin Tughlaq. They were converted to Islam and sent back to restore the sultan's authority. Harihara did that, but the temptation to found a kingdom of his own proved irresistible. In 1336, Harihara crowned himself king of Hastinavati, what is now modern Hampi. He and his brother

Bukka managed to revert to Hinduism despite caste laws. This was quite a feat. They managed to get the backing of a religious leader, Vidyaranya, who, in the manner of religious leaders, found a foolproof explanation. Harihara was the vice-regent of the local deity Virupaksha; whatever had divine sanction could hardly be questioned. And the site chosen for the new kingdom's capital was holy ground: the goddess Pampa had married Shiva on the riverbank; and parts of the epic Ramayana had taken place in its hills and caves.

Explanations that allude to divinity, human or otherwise, tend to be persuasive. Epics are equally compelling. Vijayanagar became the capital of the kingdom it gave its name to. What followed was one of the greatest urban expressions of the relationship between men and gods. Through the media of war, worship, and the rituals of power, the ancient Hindu ideals of kingship were resurrected.

The kingdom grew into an empire; conquest extended its borders. There were many enemies: the kings of Andhra, the coastal kingdoms, and most of all, the permanent northern enemy of the Muslim kingdoms. A permanent enemy meant elaborate defense arrangements, and the necessity for revenue. The cavalry was improved by importing horses (first from the Arabs, then from the Portuguese traders in Goa) and drafting Turkish mercenaries. Vijayanagar's wealth was based on a control of the lucrative spice trade of the south and cotton trade of the southeast, and administered by an able bureaucracy. Forests were cleared, new land settled, large irrigation tanks built, and dams constructed across rivers, involving considerable hydraulic engineering. The city became the nucleus of the Vijayanagar Empire, the dominant power in South India for two centuries.

Much remains as witness to this past. The halls and baths, the numerous monolithic sculptures, even the king's balance, where kings are said to have been weighed against gold or grain which was then distributed among the poor. All tell a familiar tale of epic proportion, but one in which beauty is inseparable from wealth and power. As always, official beauty and grandeur have a dark and ugly underside. I did not see Suban again, and I did not get a chance to tell him that.

The day I was to leave Hampi, I walked alone past a well-tended field of horse gram, a spread of purple flowers between the Sarasvati temple and the octagonal bath. I met a group of young men from nearby Hospet in the Ramachandra temple; they confided they were there to look at the art students, girls from Bombay and Baroda with sketchbooks and paintboxes. In the chariot street of the Virupaksha temple, the stone stalls used by merchants and pilgrims now housed villagers, beggars, a cycle shop, and a homeopathic clinic. Behind this temple which predates the empire, I saw women patting cow dung into cakes, a girl chasing the hens away from the eggs they had laid, and a cluster of huts. This was Hampi village. I bought myself idlis; I looked at all the autos I passed in case Suban was in one of them. As I walked back to the hotel, a group of children in school uniforms waylaid me, asking for pens. It made sense to me, their clamor for pens. Despite all the accounts of Vijayanagar, the story remains incomplete. The city—splendor, ruin, tourist trap—is not yet done with its chroniclers.

Some cities of victory are in ruins; but other cities have sprung up to sing the same strange song of triumph.

There is another city of showy monuments far away in another time. The city, Washington, D.C., holds the white building that was, like so many powerful symbols of brick and mortar, built by outsiders—stonemasons recruited from as far away as Edinburgh, and slaves hired from their owners. The White House personifies world power, and what this power is capable of doing to the rest of the world. It is a building that evokes awe and patriotism, or anger and contempt, in equal measure.

WASHINGTON 2004, 1997:
FULL AND HALF-FULL ID CHECKS

It was April in Washington, a good time for flowering shrubs. I walked past the White House several times. More than the familiar domed building in the distance, my eye was caught by the splashes of yellow forsythia neatly pruned and caged in.

But once I stood at the gates, the building took over. The entire area had an air of holding its breath. Gates, guards, and guns told me that this is an Important Place where I had to be on my best diffident behavior. They told me that this place, like other symbols of ruling might, needed to awe spectators and diminish them. The official boards added to the feeling of standing before a sanctum sanctorum. *VIP Passing* said one. *100% ID check* said another. I put my hand in my bag, touched my Indian passport for reassurance.

Tourists, mostly American, stood at the gates, peeping in. A man selling guides to the White House and its neighborhood did brisk business. Cameras flashed and clicked every other minute. I watched some of the tourists ready with their cameras, on the alert, waiting for something to happen or someone important to show up. After all, there are only so many pictures even a tourist can take of the grounds and the building in the distance. Earlier I had noticed several American-size squirrels chasing each other round the trees. Now one of them ran up to the gates and settled itself comfortably on its haunches, a large nut in its paws. The squirrel eating its nut without self-consciousness was an ideal photo-op. "A White House squirrel!" laughed a couple of the tourists. Despite the laughter, digital cameras took aim purposefully. The White House squirrel, acclimatized to its surroundings, gamely presented its best side for posterity.

The White House is, of course, *the* superpower in the city. But the city is also lined with other buildings, one impervious building after the other with various instruments of power within their walls. There is, for example, the granite Greek revival structure that is the oldest "departmental building" in the city; it still serves as the headquarters for the treasury department. This building, I was told, has the "1864 burglar-proof vault," but public tours of the building have been suspended since 9/11. And here and there are the memorials. Some flaunt their official importance; some are almost hidden away; others are in the nature of graffiti—posters and souvenir shops attuned to what the people are meant to remember. Together, these memorials speak eloquently of how the city may be seen, and how the city sees itself.

* * *

It was not my first visit to Washington. That happened in 1977 when I was a graduate student in America. An older classmate of mine heard I was planning a trip with a friend. She generously told me that she had a house in Washington, and though the place had an old Filipino called Packy as a house-sitter, there was more than enough room for the three of us. I spoke to the house-sitter on the phone; he was delighted, especially when he heard that I had once lived in Manila. But when we met face to face, he was far from delighted. He stared past me, his face fixed in shock. Packy was looking at my friend, an African American.

The irony was that Packy's neighborhood was by no means an all-white neighborhood. What torments the man must have suffered every day, locking himself in, afraid of skins a few shades darker than his. As an Indian, I recognized his shade-fear immediately—I had already had unsolicited advice from a number of Indian well-wishers about how I should avoid the black parts of the city, whether in New York or Washington. Perhaps I am being too kind to Packy, whose real name (Paco? Pacheco?) I never found out. One night, Packy confided that all the whites in his neighborhood were white trash.

It was, on the whole, an uncomfortable visit. Coming home in the evening meant returning to an air thick with the tension of the unsaid. As a child in a Bombay school, I had puzzled for days about Countee Cullen's poem "The Incident." Despite living

63

in a country with caste, I was unable to understand what racism did, even to children. All these years later, fancying myself a young woman of the world, I was still astounded when I first felt the small pinpricks of racism.

My friend must have been uncomfortable, but he decided to ignore it. We pretended the old man's fear and distaste was not real if we did not talk about it. But one night, as we walked home from dinner at a Vietnamese restaurant, we began talking about Washington. About a city that became a center of the civil rights movement; a city with a large black population from the time it was built.

Not only was Washington built with the labor of black and foreign hands, the city received thousands of black Americans from the south from World War I to long after World War II. The black citizens of Washington form the majority; the inner city of the white city of power has remained black. But the heart of Washington, the White House, was out of bounds to most blacks till the end of the nineteenth century. One exception was the "egg-rolling ceremony" black children could take part in once a year. Though it was illegal for them to work or play with white children in schools, libraries, and playgrounds, they could "integrate" with the children of regular citizens on Easter Day.

Vijayanagar, Washington. How is a great city born? How does it grow in turn into an empire? For a city to be built, for it to grow into a city of victory, a few declarations of independence are essential as its beginnings. The Hampi area could not have become Vijayanagar without Bukka and Harihara declaring independence from Delhi in 1336 and building a sanctified Hindu genealogy. More than four centuries later in 1792, the cornerstone of the capital on the Potomac River could not have been laid without declaring independence from the king in London.

Whether Washington or its surrogate Philadelphia, sometimes, in the same city, very different sorts of declarations had to be made.

1776, 1796: DECLARATIONS OF INDEPENDENCE

It is 1776. The summer night in Philadelphia is uncomfortably warm and humid. On the second floor of Graff House, rented from the brick mason Jacob Graff, Thomas Jefferson is hard at work at his desk. He bends over the mess of papers, deliberating. He knows he will have to write and rewrite till he gets it right. He can make the words flow, but will they be powerful enough to take on the two objects they race toward? His words must help flare into being a revolutionary war; they must make it crystal clear that an armed revolt by the thirteen colonies against King George is the only way forward. His words must also conjure up a dream of radical ideas. A dream of a new nation supported by the righteous pillars of political rights, full citizenship, justice, democracy. (And slavery? That too must be addressed, but how?)

The day has been a long one; too many people, too many voices. Too many words, spoken and written. The days have been like this for a while. How long it has been since he had a quiet lazy day of cooking a meal, making some new wine—he puts down his pen, stretches, yawns. His shoulders ache. His concentration broken, he can sense someone hovering in the background. But he doesn't turn to look. Who can it be but faithful Richard? Richard, of all his hundreds of slaves, whom he has taken along with him to so many places. And indeed, seeing his master pause, Richard comes forward, takes away the empty cup, replaces it with a fresh cup of tea just the way his master likes it. Richard retires but does not leave the room. He remains somewhere in the background, in case he should be needed again. He knows, though he was born a slave, that his master is writing about *independence*; that he is not just writing about it, but *declaring* it. Jefferson takes the cup to his lips; the hot sweet tea goes down his throat like a potion of strength. He thinks for a moment of Richard waiting quietly behind him, a slave waiting on his master who is writing the Declaration of Independence. Then the tea goes to work; Jefferson bends over his task again.

The words are now building their own grand scheme, their own great city of democracy. He writes: "We hold these truths to be self-evident, that all men are created equal, that they are endowed by their Creator with certain unalienable Rights, that among these are Life, Liberty and the pursuit of Happiness."

Jefferson reads the lines, grunts with satisfaction. They will do.

Jefferson has just lived through the defining moment of his life. These lines of his will become famous; more famous than Jefferson, who will become the third president of the nation he is helping create. Those planning the French Revolution will be inspired by them. Even the Vietnamese (who will, much later, have a close encounter with Americans) will find these lines helpful as they fight the French colonialists.

The silent Richard, too, will get a bit role in history. He will become an African American witness to the writing of a historical document of freedom—though he is only a valued slave, and remembered mainly by African Americans looking for their share of the past in the history of American democracy. But before that, other blacks fighting against slavery will use Jefferson's lines to support their cause: luckily, the Declaration of Independence does not actually sanction slavery. Though it does not clearly support its abolition, it can be read, if it needs to be, as looking ahead to a future without slavery.[4]

* * *

Twenty years after Jefferson's evening with the Declaration, faithful Richard hovering behind his master, it is summer again.

It is May in Philadelphia; the year, 1796. The young light-skinned slave with freckles on her face does not know what year it is. But she knows it is time to make her move. The master and mistress are at dinner. Soon they will expect her to come in, clear the dishes.

Free. What a word it is, a little sound like the exhalation of breath. But once it is hers, she can stop holding her breath. *Free.* Maybe this simple word burning like a flame in her heart will lead her out of this house. A house in which the most powerful man in the country lives.

The house is the Executive Mansion in Philadelphia. (The White House is a work in progress.) The master is George

Washington; the mistress Martha Custis Washington. The slave is Ona Maria Judge, who came to the Washington household when she was about ten years old, as a dower slave on loan from the Custis estate.

Ona has always worked in the house, never in the field. She has spun thread; she has woven cloth; she has churned butter; she has turned tallow into soap; she has dipped candles; she has washed laundry; she has cooked. Then, like her mother Betty, Ona has learned to sew. She was so good at it that her Master once described her as a "perfect Mistress of her needle." Her mistress made Ona her personal maid, her "body servant."

But all that is over. Her life will change soon because of the President. Master George does not want to stand for another term and the Washingtons are already packing to go home to Virginia. A while back, Mistress Martha told Ona that she will make a fine wedding gift to Martha's granddaughter. Ona knows it is now or maybe never.

Ona leaves the back door from the kitchen ajar. If she fails, she could pretend she forgot some washing outside. Or that the cat was mewing at the door. Or—but she won't fail because she refuses to. She has already left her bag, a small bag of her worldly belongings, with free friends in the city. Her friends must be waiting for her. She glides ghostlike across the dark backyard, and then she is out. She pauses, looks at the street ahead, mysterious in twilight. She does not look back. She runs down the streets, a flying dark phantom who will become a real person once she is aboard Captain Bowles' *Nancy*.

She knows Portsmouth, New Hampshire, is no paradise.

Her friends have warned her that she could be caught. She will be a permanent fugitive, wherever she is in America, even in "free" states. Captain Bowles, her friends, they could all become criminals because of her.

* * *

Master George knows about owning slaves. After all, he owned his first ten slaves when he was eleven years old. (At his death the revolutionary war general, founding father, and first president of the United States would own more than three hundred men, women, and children. He did not free a single slave in his lifetime.) Washington wrote in 1786:

> I can only say that there is not a man living who wishes more sincerely than I do, to see a plan adopted for the abolition of [slavery]—but there is only one proper and effectual mode by which it can be accomplished, & that is by Legislative authority: and this, as far as my suffrage will go, shall never be wanting. But when slaves who are happy & content to remain with their present masters, are tampered with & seduced to leave them; when masters are taken at unawar[e]s by these practices; when a conduct of this sort begets discontent on one side and resentment on the other, & when it happens to fall on a man whose purse will not measure with that of the Society, & he loses his property for want of means to defend it—it is oppression in the latter case, & not humanity in any; because it introduces more evils than it can cure.[5]

Yes, he has spoken of slavery as an evil; and Master George has, after all, hundreds of other slaves; but how can he let Ona go? Martha and he have treated Ona with kindness. Martha misses her privileged house slave. Doesn't Ona owe them some loyalty? In late May 1796, an advertisement for a runaway slave appears in *The Pennsylvania Gazette*:

> Absconded from the household of the President of the United States, ONA JUDGE, a light mulatto girl, much freckled, with very black eyes and bushy hair. She is of middle stature, slender, and delicately formed, about twenty years of age. She has many changes of good clothes, of all sorts, but they are not sufficiently recollected to be described—As there was no suspicion of her going off, nor no provocation to do so, it is not easy to conjecture whither she has gone, or fully, what her design is; but as she may attempt to escape by water, all masters of vessels are cautioned against admitting her into them, although it is probable she will attempt to pass for a free woman, and has, it is said, where-withal to pay her passage. Ten dollars will be paid to any person who will bring her home, if taken in the city, or on board any vessel in the harbor;—and a reasonable additional sum if apprehended at, and brought from a greater distance, and in proportion to the distance.[6]

Meanwhile, Ona goes to work. She works at her sewing; she makes new friends among the blacks in Portsmouth, and they ease her way to an almost free life. But her past—and her owners—do not leave her alone. As she hurries down a street, she is recognized by a friend of the Washingtons. The Washingtons soon know where she is. If caught, she, like other captured runaway slaves, may be demoted to working in the fields; she may be beaten, even executed. Maybe she is being unfair, thinking like that. Master and Mistress (she corrects herself, Mr. and Mrs. Washington) have never been unkind to her. But no, kind or not, she will not be caught. She will not become a slave again, even to "good" slave owners.

Washington writes to Joseph Whipple, Collector of Customs in Portsmouth. (The Whipples are an important and well-known family of the Revolution.) The letter demands that Whipple seize Ona and put her "on board a Vessel bound immediately" to either Mount Vernon or Alexandria. Washington adds, "The ingratitude of the girl, who was brought up and treated more like a child than a Servant (and [given] Mrs. Washington's desire to recover her) ought not to escape with impunity if it can be avoided."

Whipple warns that abduction can cause a riot, such is the power of the abolitionists in Portsmouth. The matter must be taken care of more tactfully. Whipple offers Ona a job and interviews her. Though he senses her "thirst for compleat freedom" he almost convinces her that she should return to the Washingtons. She will be freed when they die. But a friend helps Ona see through the ruse and she turns down the offer.

Washington is enraged. Such unfaithfulness deserves punishment, but he sends his nephew, Burnwell Bassett Jr., to

Portsmouth to make a generous gesture. Ona will be freed once back in Virginia. Ona's reply is brief and categorical: "I am free now and choose to remain so." There is no choice but to bring her back by force. But Ona goes into hiding. Three months later, Washington is dead.

Ona outlived Washington by fifty years. She married a sailor, Jack Staines, and they had three children. Her interviews in the abolitionist newspapers *The Granite Freeman* in 1845, and *The Liberator* in 1847, described the Washingtons and what she thought of slavery; her escape and the attempts to capture her; and how proud she felt on finally learning to read.

Ona's life continued to be difficult; in some ways, even more difficult than it was as a slave. Poverty followed her and her family till the end. Such was this poverty that Ona's daughters may have been hired out as indentured servants. But when asked if she regretted leaving the Washingtons since she had to work harder than ever, she said, "No, I am free, and have, I trust, been made a child of God by the means." Though she remained a fugitive, Ona was never a slave again.

* * *

"I, too, am America," Langston Hughes said in his poem "I, Too, Sing America." Over the hard years, the negroes turned into blacks, then African Americans and people of color. They too have been called upon to help the great city expand; or to go to war to defend, or invade, or conquer.

Washington is, as the brochures say, where the nation commemorates the wars the country has fought and "the men and

72

women who served and gave their lives in them." In 2004, I was warned that I would not be able to see the Washington monument since it was currently undergoing "site improvements to enhance security." As I walked away from the White House, I saw a straight pillar of smooth granite with a gilt angel on top holding the American flag. The plaque read, "Memorial Association of the first division and patriotic friends to the memory of the dead of the division who gave their lives in the world war that the liberty and the ideals of our country might endure." Nearby, easy to mistake for a side wall, was a more modest memorial to Vietnam veterans. The plaque, less effusive, said, "To the soldiers of the first infantry division, US army, who made the supreme sacrifice in Vietnam." In between these two memorials was another, even easier to miss. A patch of orderly red tulips and a small plaque raised on the ground made a brief reference to the "supreme sacrifice in Desert Storm (Iraq and Saudi Arabia) 1991."

But the living monument to Vietnam veterans in the Constitution Gardens, the National Vietnam Veterans Memorial, evoked a very different atmosphere. After the old-world statues and angels, this memorial had a contemporary feel to it. Wreaths and flowers were sold in stalls; schoolchildren lined up to buy these and a variety of stickers to "thank a vet today for your freedom."

Black marble panels stood one after the other to make a wall. The panels were covered with names. A large number of the names were of ridiculously young men: I counted quite a number who "died with honor for God, country and corps" at age twenty and twenty-one. In addition to flowers, there were all kinds of personal mementoes placed at the feet of the panels. A medal with the card attached to it reading "To my brother George"; letters to a Roy, beginning "You may be gone, but we never..." There was also the occasional wooden dove painted gray and white. As I read the names on the panels, I overheard an old woman behind me asking the young man with her: "All these names. Are they people in Vietnam who died?" "No, Mom," I heard him reply impatiently. "These are Americans."

Perhaps Mom would have had no trouble understanding the unambiguous souvenir shops outside the Lincoln Memorial. These were works in progress of a nation at war. The stars-and-stripes stickers for sale warned that "these colors don't run. Flag burners, beware!" One poster which sold briskly said, "Iraqi Most Wanted." Below this caption was a hand of cards; each card had a face and name. Saddam was the ace of spades. One card, a joker, listed the Iraqi military ranks; the other joker listed titles in Arabic transcribed in English. Several cards had a scrawl across the face: "Gotcha!" One quiet brown poster, which looked like an official tag, the kind attached to suitcases in airports, read "USA Permit No. 91101. Terrorist Hunting Permit. No Bag Limit—Tagging Not Required."

Advice from the past had been resurrected to use the newly renewed hunting permit. There was an informative notice on the marines from a Rear Admiral Jay R. Stark of the US Navy dated November 1995: "Marines I see as two breeds, Rottweilers or Dobermans, because marines come in two varieties, big and mean, or skinny and mean. They're aggressive on the attack and tenacious on defense. They've got really short hair and they always go for the throat."

With this advice in mind, it was a little difficult to make the journey back in time and enter the nearby Lincoln Memorial. I hung about outside where tourist kiosks sold FBI and CIA sweatshirts and headbands. I did a quick survey; all of them were manned (or womanned) by Vietnamese.

* * *

The Lincoln Memorial is a pillared Greek temple of sorts with a large statue of Lincoln sitting on a chair. He is formally dressed, the bow tie tightly in place. He sits straight, almost stiff. (It reminded me of my grandfather's generation. No one believed in smiling for photographs then; images for posterity were taken seriously.) Like my grandfather, he is unsmiling, this Lincoln. Maybe he is considering the circumstances that forced him into taking action against the legal right of his white fellow citizens to enslave blacks. His mind must almost be made up. His hands, the most human part of the statue, look ready to move any minute. Or maybe he is recalling that speech of his on the evening of April 11, 1865 when he stood on the White House balcony. He had spoken about ways to reconstruct the nation once the defeated Confederate states were back in the union. One way to imagine the nation afresh, he had said, was to extend the vote to blacks—at least some of them.

There was a man listening to him, an angry man called John Wilkes Booth, an actor and a Confederate sympathizer. Three days later, Booth shot Lincoln while he was watching a play at the Ford Theater. A massive manhunt was launched with as many as ten thousand federal troops, detectives, and police. When he finally died of a gunshot wound, Booth was supposed to have said something to the effect of "Tell my mother I die for my country." Booth loved his native South as it was, slavery and all; and the Presidential promise of voting rights for blacks would change his home beyond recognition.

(What would Booth feel if he could time travel to 2008, see the first black president installed in the White House? Would he take heart from the fact that the ground realities have not really changed? Would he feel vindicated that milestones have not altered how African Americans, Arabs, Muslims and foreigners are seen?)

Lincoln sits still, larger than life in a dramatically lit memorial. The carved letters on a side wall declare, in words that speak the language of a city of victory. "Four score and seven years ago our father brought forth on this continent a new nation, conceived in liberty, and dedicated to the proposition that all men are created equal..." Then I notice that on either side of his statue are small signs that seem to whisper from backstage: "Quiet: Respect please!"

3

TODA CAFÉ BLUES

OOTY / OOTACAMUND / UDHAGAI / UDHAGAMANDALAM, 2008

The sky is a deep uncompromising blue, completely cloudless. From the top of the hill I have climbed, the world is open sky and wave after wave of terraced hills. For a city slick, Ooty is still a queen. The panoramic view from the hilltop holds me in thrall for several blessed minutes before I remember the Ooty I knew; and more disturbing, before I get a glimpse of the many old and new Ootys my companion knows.

The view may be spectacular, Ooty may still be a queen, but she is a sad old queen with too many names. Like many old queens, she has a checkered past; skeletons spill out of her closet. The woman standing by me as I look at the sweep of hills could have been this dispossessed queen in flesh and blood. She's a Toda woman in her fifties, dressed in a traditional stark white shawl embroidered with red and black buffalo horns, hill flowers, even, perhaps, some of the lost tales of her tribe.

Her name is Paksin. Sin, she tells me, means gold in the Toda language.

Paksin and her husband live in a traditional Toda hut; there are three of these curved huts in this *mund*, the Toda village on

79

top of the Ooty Botanical Gardens. Two of the huts are homes, and the third, which sits alone at some distance enclosed by a low brick wall, is a temple. A government-type sign stuck on the brick wall says "*No inside permitted.*" The government is everywhere in and around the mund. It's there in the caricature plaster of Paris Toda standing like a desolate saint in his grotto on the hillside as you make your way to the mund. This plaster Toda has wisps of black wool stuck to his chin. His back is hunched as if he has not learned to walk upright yet. And once you're in the mund, the government's there in the bleak barrack-like houses that have been built for the villagers. The two "real" Toda huts are for tourists to see. Paksin and her husband are Todas who live "like Todas" so the government can preserve and protect and sell heritage.

* * *

Once upon a time, this hilly place within arm's reach of the heavens was home to the pastoral Todas and other tribes—the Badaga agriculturalists, the Kota artisans and the Kurumba food-gatherers and sorcerers. The hills were too steep, and the plateau too cold, for much interaction with the plains people, mostly Hindus. Though isolated together in the Nilgiri Hills, and though many of their villages were within walking distance of each other, the four tribes spoke different languages, both literally and otherwise. Toda life was centered on buffalo herds; Kota life on the smithy; Badaga life on crops; and the Kurumbas were in the jungle except when they visited their clients in other tribes to deliver magical services. In 1941, American anthropologist David Mandelbaum wrote of the formal nature of these interactions: "whenever a Kurumba comes into view, the word flashes through the village, women and children run for the safety of home, cower inside till the Kurumbas have gone. All transactions... take place outside the village limits."[1] Similarly, Kota musicians were compulsory in important Toda ceremonies. But if the musicians came too near the dairy, the place was polluted, and would have to go through an elaborate purification ritual. Given these defined minglings, all intimate contact was taboo.

Then everything changed in ways not even the best magician among the Kurumbas could have foreseen.

* * *

Paksin and her husband seem to be alone in the mund. It's not tourist season, and most of the Todas in the mund have gone to a wedding. Paksin invites me to enter the traditional semi-barrel-shaped hut the government has built for her. She bends and slips in through the small entrance; I follow her. It is a neat little place inside. We sit on the single cot there and talk. Unlike many of the other munds, there's not much land here that has been allotted to the Todas for cultivation. At any rate, Paksin and her husband do not have any. She looks toward the open door, which frames a stretch of hills.

"They gave it all away," she says. "All our lands, all the slopes you can see from here. For an anna, even half an anna." (I was only three years old when the anna coins fell out of usage. But the word continued to be used in my childhood—twenty-five paise made four annas, and fifty paise eight annas.) But Paksin is talking of much earlier times—colonial times—though she makes it sound like it happened yesterday.

She doesn't know who he is, but Paksin's words make me imagine John Sullivan, "founder" of Ooty, discovering the "Neilgherry" hills with his friends, dreaming of sanatoriums and lakes, stone houses and churches, in a cool air almost like home. I can imagine Paksin's pastoral ancestors, considering the swathes of forested land about them, taking it for granted because there's so much of it, enough for everyone. No one at the time—not the most benevolent or visionary of the Englishmen, nor the shrewdest of the Todas—could have had an inkling of the melancholy that would henceforth weigh down this mountain air.

NILGIRIS, 1819: THE FATHER OF OOTACAMUND

It is January 2, 1819. John Sullivan, along with a group of Englishmen and Indian Sepoys, is exploring the Nilgiris—the Blue Mountains—to find out if the fabulous tales he has heard about the place are true. The best part of the expedition is that this break from a collector's life on the plains is considered work. All he has to do is send a report to his employers, the East India Company.

Sullivan was fifteen when he first came to India as a "writer" for the East India Company. This may not have been an accident; his grandfather, Lawrence Sullivan, was a director of the company. In 1817 the writer became the permanent collector of Coimbatore District. (Coimbatore, where I was born less than one and a half centuries later, is supposed to have been a jungle village headed by an Irula chieftain. Much later it came to be known as the Manchester of India.)

The mountains Sullivan and his party climb exhale a blue smoky haze; it could be from the eucalyptus trees that grow everywhere. Or it could be the flowers on the slopes—what they will later discover is *kurunji*, the flower which blooms once every twelve years. Sullivan likes this tale. He has chosen the right year—it makes him feel his visit was meant to be. And flowers or no flowers, he likes the air. It is cool, as cool and misty as London.

It is also a bracing adventure. The terrain they have to cross is rough; the precipices they encounter are steep; and there is always the fear of wild animals. Six days later, by the time they set up camp in Dimbhatti, just north of Kotagiri, some of his men are dead. But Sullivan's heart swells with the deep breath of mountain air he takes in. He, John, is about to plant the British flag in a clearing amid the trees. And besides, he has fallen in love.

* * *

Later he wrote to Thomas Munro (of whom we will hear again) of the Neilgherry hills: "This is the finest country ever… it resembles I suppose Switzerland more than any other part of Europe… the hills [are] beautifully wooded and [there is a] fine strong spring with running water in every valley."

Sullivan's life became bound with the bit of Europe he found in South India. He made it his business to campaign for the Nilgiris as a "resort of Invalids" given its "unusually temperate and healthy" climate in a country which was, for Englishmen anyway, unusually hot and unhealthy. Sullivan was no invalid. What he wanted was a summer residence, and he wanted other officials to join the English settlement he could visualize on the endless stretches of land. He went back to Dimbhatti and bought land from the Todas at one rupee an acre; it was surprisingly easy. He had a house built—Stonehouse, it was called. He called it a cottage, but the natives took to calling this first European house in the area Kal-Bungla, or Stone Bungalow. His wife was the first white woman the natives saw. Henrietta Cecilia moved into Stonehouse in 1823 with her infant son. Then others, including Sullivan's correspondent Thomas Munro, now Sir Munro and governor of Madras, moved to Ootacamund.

The story goes that the Badagas, the first natives Sullivan met, "explained" the Todas to him. He was told that every Toda mund or settlement had a single stone: *otta-kal*. So the place became Otta-kal-mund. Sullivan liked the sound and the explanation. But all he could get round his tongue was Ootacamund. No matter, thought the new Father of Ootacamund, the name could always be shortened to Ooty.

Sullivan now owned vast tracts of land, many times more than all the other European settlers put together. He had an impressive house (or cottage). Hunting was excellent—the place teemed with game and wildfowl. Other Englishmen seeking rest cures or R & R were his neighbors. He planted an oak that would survive the centuries and be called Sullivan's Oak.

But John Sullivan was too enterprising to be content. The place needed some English crops, churches, graveyards; maybe a lake. Sullivan went back to work. He pushed for the construction of the early ghat roads up into the hills. He introduced tea, which would later define the Nilgiris commercially; European varieties of wheat and barley; potatoes, cabbage, radish, turnips; peaches, apples, and strawberries—"English vegetables and fruit." The serpentine Ooty Lake was created among groves of eucalyptus by damming the mountain streams flowing down the valley. Gardens were set out. Official buildings and churches were built—some with material plundered from Tipu Sultan's Lal Bagh Palace in Srirangapatna, which the British called Seringapatam.

What was he like, this John Sullivan? He invited the disapproval of the British authorities by advocating that the "natives should be entrusted with a great share in the administration of their own affairs." Yet he used his government position to amass enormous personal wealth. In 1880, in *A Manual of the Nilgiri District in the Madras Presidency*, H.B. Grigg described Sullivan as a friend of the native who insisted that the Todas had proprietary rights over the lands in the Nilgiris plateau, and that they must receive compensation for any land acquired from them. Maybe Sullivan forgot how cheaply he got his own lands.

The plan—to make of this bit of Indian land "an England in the tropics" in which "the whole of the grounds" are "to be laid down with English grass"—had more or less worked. Not only was Sullivan's dream of making Ooty a sanatorium for British troops realized, Ooty also became a military cantonment in 1828. This meant Sullivan was no longer in charge; his rival, Major William Kelso, took over. Ooty became the summer capital of the Madras presidency. The fresh air and the deep green valleys Sullivan had fallen in love with now gave Ooty a British title: Queen of Hill Stations.

Sullivan was no longer the only white sahib in charge, but he wasn't done with Ooty. Once he finished his tenure as collector of Coimbatore, he came back as the senior member of the Board of Revenue of the Madras presidency. But in 1841, his wife Henrietta and his daughter Harriet died within ten days of each other. Mother and daughter were buried in a cemetery that may still be seen, an overgrown but pretty place behind St. Stephen's Church, a cathedral built exclusively for the British. Sullivan finally left for England with his remaining eight children. We don't know how long he grieved for Henrietta, Harriet, or Ooty. In his only surviving photograph he is rather large, and rather sullen. His grave is in Berkshire, not Ooty, and it is shared by his second wife, Frances.

There is no memorial to John Sullivan in Ooty. But, says anthropologist and Nilgiris expert Paul Hockings, "his memorial is... everywhere" in Ooty.

Ootacamund continued to be queen. In his *Ootacamund: A History*, published in 1908, Sir Fredrick Price approvingly quotes from Lord Lytton's letter to his wife: Ooty has "such beautiful *English* rain, such delicious *English* mud... Imagine Hertfordshire lanes, Devonshire downs, Westmoreland lakes, Scotch trout streams, and Lusitanian views!" The settlers also had a railway, a hospital, and twenty-two acres of botanical gardens, with an ancient fossilized tree and a collector's trove of exotic and indigenous plants, shrubs, ferns, and trees. A Captain Douglas responded to the need for the English to have a "common meeting ground," and with "zeal, energy and perseverance" founded the Ootacamund Club in 1841. The white Ooty-ites could now play snooker surrounded by hunting trophies, or sit down to dinner in their formal jackets at the Planter's Ball. It was home. It was better than home.

* * *

While the new Ooty-ites were eating dinner off silver dishes with Mappin and Webb cutlery, what were Paksin's ancestors doing? The Todas, and their Badaga, Kurumba, and Kota neighbors?

With the British—the officials, the soldiers, the missionaries, and the holidaymakers—arrived a gaggle of lowlanders. These newcomers were servants, merchants, "wanderers looking for a living." They were Hindu, Muslim, or Christian; of many castes and regions.

The tribes began to go to the weekly market, where they saw strange goods and customs. Some even saw a movie or two. Their fields saw a brief battle waged between the old millet and barley, and the new tea and potatoes. Over their huts, ancient thatch fought a losing battle against tiled roofs. The new won every time. But the old was not entirely discouraged. The Todas—Paksin's forefathers—found that some of their villages were within the limits of the largest English settlement. The "natives," the "aboriginals," the "tribals," became a sight that must be seen and photographed by every English newcomer. (The rajas did one better; a few Todas became "ornamental guards" for some palaces.) The souls of the Todas were not neglected either. A special mission was set up to save them. Those who converted remained on friendly terms with the rest of the tribe, but lived apart.

The world of the Nilgiri tribals grew. As it grew, it cracked here and there; old Otta-kal-mund fell into the dark crevices. The unseen English queen and her representative, the British administrator, now had the last word in the queen of hill stations, not the tribal headmen. Even the gods and their priests shook before this new power. The villagers of Kotagiri, for instance, discovered this when they lost their home and got a new home like a consolation prize.

* * *

The villagers of Kotagiri lived in a particularly beautiful spot, and the Englishmen bought as much land as they could in this place, "the mountain of Kotas." They built their bungalows, police station, bazaar, and hotels around the village. But the English discovered there was a snake—or a smell—in the paradise they had built. An informant told Mandelbaum in 1941: "The jungle people, the Kotas, used to go out of the village and in the night [and] just sit wherever they wish[ed]." In other words, they answered the calls of nature amid nature. The colonial administration built two latrines for the Kotas, one for men and one for women; the villagers were ordered to make use of them. But such a change could not happen without divine sanction. The priests, headmen, and diviners among the Kotas consulted the "*pembacol*, the woman who becomes possessed to the music of the lute." The lute-woman vetoed the latrines: the smell of the latrines would offend the village gods. The tribal council had no option but to move the entire village. The two priests of the village chose different sites. For the first time in the living memory of the Kotas, the two village deities were separated and the village divided. There was great misery till the English, who had started it all in the first place, solved the problem. The Court chose a third site, midway between the places the warring priests had selected. The villagers of Kotagiri had to make a new hill of Kotas there, leaving the "civilized" latrines behind.

Unlike the Kotas, many Badagas embraced the changes that came with the outsiders. Of all the tribes, they felt closest to the caste Hindus from the plains. Now, with greater contact with plains culture, they began to look afresh at their own customs. For instance: music was central to Badaga rituals and they had always had Kota musicians perform at these ceremonies. But now, with caste on their minds, they began to suspect that musicians were, as a group, beyond the pale. The pro-change Badagas wanted their rituals to do away with music altogether. The traditionalists were incensed; they would not give up their old links with the Kotas. Pro-music and anti-music factions clashed and several Badagas were killed in the process.

* * *

But Paksin and I cannot stay too long in the times of our ancestors' follies, or their innocence and defeat. The present—personified by two ubiquitous creatures, the government and the rich outsider—intrudes into our conversation.

Paksin has four daughters and two sons. Not one of them finished school; and not one of them works the land. Two of them are tailors; the rest work at any job they can get, in the hundreds of small shops scattered across the hills. Her husband is sick, she doesn't know with what. The government has been of no help with her children's schooling or jobs, or her husband's illness. The government has only built their houses in the mund.

Maybe Paksin is beginning to feel guilty about this sorrowful litany of complaints. Maybe she's remembered she's supposed to be showing visitors like me the Toda way of life. But when she turns into a tour guide, I hear another roll call of deprivations. Toda women, she says, are not allowed to step into the temple; in fact, they are not allowed to leave the enclosure around the hut from the front gate. They have to use the side or the back to keep up tradition. The Todas made all kinds of silver and bead jewelry at one time; but now those skills have more or less died with "the grandfathers." The outsiders, she says, design them, make them, and sell them as souvenirs.

All this time, Paksin's husband has not said a word to me. He sits outside the hut, a morose old man trying to warm up in the sunshine. He's not exactly old; he's just been retired from his job as a gardener in the botanical gardens.

I see his ex-colleagues at work as I make my way down from the mund through the gardens. Near the dragon tree from the

Canary Islands and the monkey puzzle tree from Australia, there's a small pond, and several gardeners are trimming the borders of foliage. Keeping them company is a plaster of Paris crocodile lying at the edge of the pond, its jaws wide open in devilish glee. As a counterpoint to this *jungli* specimen, an overweight plaster nymph stands in the middle of the pond. She pours imaginary water.

I can picture officials in a government office, deciding over cups of too-sweet tea, that that these trees, nymphs, and crocodiles are all educational. I can see one of them, a prim man with a neat paunch, interrupting to ask, "But what is education without Rules?" This sage of unhappy classrooms has his way. At the entrance of the gardens, boards on either side wag an admonishing finger. Don't spit. Don't pluck the flowers. Don't litter. Don't make noise. Don't cook. Don't smoke. Don't drink. Don't disturb others. Don't make nuisance. Don't. Don't.

* * *

The next day, a friend's driver, a handsome and chatty young man called Senthil, drove me around Ooty. Outside the botanical gardens, with no helpful rules or government huts or Toda costume-uniforms, I found it hard to identify a Toda. When I asked Senthil where the Todas were, he told me, "See that man lying on the grass sunning himself? He's lying there because he is drunk. He is a Toda." Over the half hour it took us to get to the government's Tribal Museum, a pattern emerged in Senthil's Toda-spotting. Every horizontal man we passed was supposed to be drunk, and he was supposed to be a Toda.

Senthil explained it to me kindly. The government gives the Todas so much money, they don't need to work. Senthil went on to describe a day in a Toda's life. (A man's life, I guess.) The Toda gets up in the morning and goes to the ATM; he withdraws money, he gets drunk. He lies around. When he wakes up, he is hungry, so he goes to the ATM again. He buys biryani. Once he is well fed, he wants a drink. So he goes back to the ATM, drinks, then lies around.

The government had a different script for the Todas. Having written back to the empire by changing the name of Ooty/Ootacamund to its alleged original name, Udhagai/ Udhagamandalam, the government built a museum to showcase the heritage of the Todas.

Ten kilometers from Ooty town, the Ooty Tribal Museum is in the campus of the Tribal Research Center. I had been told there are tribal huts, life-size replicas of tribals, tribal sculpture, rare photographs and artifacts of the ancient tribal groups of Tamil Nadu—what a tourist brochure calls "primitive human archaeological heritage." One of the more considerate brochures advises visitors to head for the Tribal Museum to "decrease your fatigue" and partake of "a visual snapshot tour of the various attributes of the indigenous native Toda Tribes of South India who form an important section of the Ooty society and have dwelled in Ooty for centuries even before the word 'civilization' came into existence within this Hill Station."

I walked past sculpture, tools, pots and pans, life-size trib- als standing around frozen. The photographs on the walls had helpful captions; I saw my petty government official again, an officially employed writer like John Sullivan, straining to do his job well. He must have written the caption under the photograph that affirms received wisdom—that tribal women must be photographed for their bare breasts. The caption says in bold letters, in case the photograph does not say it well enough: Tribal Woman Breast-Feeding Her Infant.

The government's museums of the Todas, made of brick, mortar, photographs, plaster of Paris, huts, and real flesh and blood, follow a precedent. The British did it first, and the model is still deeply rooted in the mind, such as it is, of the government. In colonial times,

> The English have seen to it that Toda pastures are not encroached upon, that Todas cannot sell pasture land. British motives for this consideration have been twofold; they cherish the Todas as they do ancient monuments and game preserves; secondly, the Toda pastures make excellent cover for the hunt (with jackals as quarry) which the English and the native Rajas maintain in the Nilgiris.[2]

Senthil the Toda-hunter was waiting for me outside the museum. He looked pleased when I told him I was going to the Ooty Club for lunch. It proved he was not wasting his time driving me around.

I met my lunch date in the bar of Ooty Club, a place of paneled walls, parquet flooring, rosewood furniture and brass fittings. I had been told the club was affectionately called Snooty Ooty Club, and I now saw why. My friend, whom I had never seen in anything but shorts and T-shirt, was an impeccable stranger in a long-sleeved shirt with an upright collar, a silk tie, creased trousers, and dress shoes. He was, as we used to say when we were children, suited and booted. The stiff old bartender who took my order responded to my Tamil with English. Actually, he did not take my order. Having sunk low enough in life to serve a drink to a woman, an Indian woman, a Tamil-speaking Indian woman who asked for beer, he politely assured me that what I wanted was a gimlet. I agreed; of course I must drink exactly what the clubwallas must have drunk in Sullivan's time. I was not so sure about this once I tasted the drink. The gin was fine; it was the lime cordial that took me back to the unromantic past. Lime cordial and I were old enemies. This vile synthetic mixture was given to me as a high treat in childhood, or as a soft drink to teetotaler adults.

I nursed my gimlet moodily, childish memories flooding my tongue. I looked around. We were in what was called the Mixed Bar. The lists on the walls declared the past masters of the Ootacamund Hunt; the first list was dated 1845. To remind me that I was in a Mixed Bar, there were also lists of winners of the Ladies Point to Point races. My friend told me the Gentleman's Bar behind the mixed one was the one public place in the club where the dress code is relaxed. Gentlemen, being entitled to more in life, could be seen in shirtsleeves after 8 p.m. On our way out, we took in the attractions of yet another bar—dedicated to the memory of an army captain, Colonel Jago, who introduced jackal hunting in Ooty in 1872. The bar remembered him with a painting on a wall, his riding crop encased below.

In the dining room, it was possible to live in many moments of time simultaneously—not that this is unusual in India. For the correct club-goers, there was shepherd's pie, mashed potatoes, lamb chops and roast chicken; for postcolonials, there was also South Indian, North Indian, mughlai, and Chinese. The tour after lunch was my dessert. I took in the ballroom, and the tiger, leopard, and bear skins. The heads of bison and sambhar deer stared at me glassily. (Snooty Ooty Club is also, and again affectionately, called The Morgue because of these hunting trophies.) The morgue tour included the library, which has an autographed copy of Sir Frederick Price's *Ootacamund: A History*; the reading room, which Trevor Fishlock described in his *India File* as a "a colonial treasure with a tiger skin, a carpet of character & the smell of old throne like dark leather chairs split and honed by a century's trousers"; and the Billiards Room, in which snooker was serious business since Sir Neville Chamberlain first posted its rules.

* * *

Ooty may have become Udhagamandalam,[3] a bore for non-Tamilian tongues and tourist brochures, but no matter. The place remains Ooty for everyone except the government. Instead of the Brits and the rajas, the bungalow-owners are now politicians, industrialists, corporates, and film stars. There are tourists and tourist lodges, hotels, tours, stalls and guides, honeymooners, rich boarding schoolers, and film units, so naturally there are businessmen of all sizes, shapes, and trades. Then there is the most important and motley group of carpetbaggers—the wheeler-dealers of real estate.

On the road leading away from the town, I saw a board that said *Toda Café*. The government may be dull and thick-skinned, but only the rich outsider, the real center of power in these hills, could set up a Toda Café where there's no room for Todas. It was a multi-cuisine restaurant with five-star prices. But the continental, mughlai, and Chinese food was served with the "warm hospitality of the Todas—the tribals the Nilgiris are renowned for."

I got a quick taste of this hospitality that evening after I said goodbye to Senthil and went for a long walk on the outskirts of Ooty. Just as I was feeling a little lonely—and almost missing Senthil—I came upon a cluster of homes on the slopes. It turned out to be a Badaga village, complete with a pretty little temple. As in all villages, the children made friends first. The old women followed their example. I was welcomed into every small house and conversation flowed in a friendly, natural way. For a moment, I felt quite at home; then the moment passed. The children waved at me till they were out of sight. I went on.

The sun was about to set. I could hear cowbells somewhere behind me. Ooty remained a palimpsest of loss and greed, but for now it was wearing its beautiful face again. Just then, the cowherds and their cows caught up with me. There was some discussion among the three cowherds before the oldest asked me if I was trying to decide where to buy land. I assured him I was only admiring his hills. We then walked down the road in companionable silence as the sky turned dark, and the hills a deep mysterious blue.

4

MAPPING FREEDOM

KASHMIR VIA BOMBAY AND DELHI: 1973–2011

April 2011. At the airport in Srinagar, two sets of signs greeted me. They seemed to belong to two storytellers who lived uneasily within handholding distance of each other. *Defense Airport. No photos*, announced the first storyteller. He was obviously the sort who wears a uniform day and night, breathes and dreams what he imagines is law and order. The second storyteller could also dream, but he was a failed dreamer, condemned to tired old formulas. He was incapable of irony. He could say, for example: *Welcome to Happy Valley*.

Sometimes the two storytellers collided so their signs ran into each other and they spoke at the same time. At the post of the Central Reserve Police Force, I was told, via Frost, that "The woods are lovely, dark and deep." Just in case I had trouble decoding this, there was a more matter-of-fact *Welcome to Paradise on Earth*. In the same place, at the same moment, I was warned that in this paradise on earth, I would have to *Be alert be vigilant be safe*.

Outside the airport, fifteen minutes into the visit, my first mental snapshot of Srinagar: armored cars, bunkers, and armed convoys anywhere, whether a quiet wooded lane or a busy market area; men armed and uniformed; and in the background, fuchsia and forsythia in bloom, the leaves of the chinar trees stirring in the breeze, trying to tell me something about the Kashmir I had seen before.

It was thirty-eight years since my last visit. It was possible all those years back—though it shouldn't have been—to see only the valley of happiness, a place to find peace, serenity, the entire pastoral fantasy tourist package. A place that takes you to heaven. I was seventeen when I first went to heaven in May 1973. I didn't even have to die to go there. My family packed one sweater each and we set off from Bombay for Delhi, then Kashmir.

Heaven was a couple of weeks in a houseboat on Dal Lake; it was the size of the roses; the first sight of snow; the shawls and saris passed through a ring to show us how fine they were; the food; the treks to Sonamarg and Gulmarg. It was almost like seeing close-up, but in three dimensions, what we had already seen on a flat screen.

Like most Indians, I first saw Kashmir via Bombay—the cinema that manufactured a Kashmir that existed only in the island's dream factory. There were the newsreels from Films Division, too, or the "Delhi view" of Kashmir. But these were a general blur of leaders getting off planes or out of cars, being met, inspecting this or that. Waiting impatiently for the real movie to start, the compulsory newsreel had a short shelf life in our heads.

When I try to recall what we schoolchildren in Bombay thought of Kashmir in 1965, the year of the war between India and Pakistan, I find myself drawing a blank. All I can remember is the excitement of preparing for a blackout, papering our windows with dark paper; and being told to pray for our soldiers in the school assembly. I doubt if I was more or less ignorant than any other eleven-year-old. But as far as I can remember, India and Pakistan were the players; Kashmir was barely visible in the picture we were shown.

Where we did see Kashmir was in films that were not in Delhi's black and white, but in Bombay-manufactured color. Of course, there was Nehru in Delhi, and he had said of Kashmir, "sometimes the sheer loveliness of it was overpowering and I felt faint... it seemed to me dreamlike and unreal, like the hopes and desires that fill us and so seldom find fulfillment. It was like the face of the beloved that one sees in a dream and that fades away on waking." So perhaps Delhi and Bombay agreed on one thing: it was best to relegate Kashmir to the world of dreams.

A dream of Kashmir lived on the big screen, and in the Indian imagination, endearingly pastoral, pristine, and naïve. Its shikaras floated down Dal Lake in glamorous Eastmancolor. Like snow, romance was a staple of these films. Flowers, necessary props for romance, abounded in more than the titles of films such as *Kashmir Ki Kali* and *Jab Jab Phool Khile*. In these films of the sixties, Indians tended to go to Kashmir for R & R. But sometimes, the beauty of the place also meant "waking up from a lifelong slumber" and declaring, as in the 1961 hit film *Junglee*, that love in Shimla is all very well, but "Love in Kashmir is the best."

The beauty of the valley was not only in its lakes, woods, snowy mountains, and deliciously cool weather; it also resided in the people. These Bollywood Kashmiris were rustics blessed with a noble simplicity. Unlike people in the corrupted cities the visitors came from, the locals were incapable of taking more than their due. Again and again we saw flower sellers or boatmen refusing anything beyond what they considered fair payment for their goods. Indeed, they could teach the visitor what it is to be human; or what it is, specifically, to be *Indian*. *Jab Jab Phool Khile*, released in the war-year 1965, had a boatman, an EveryRustic, as its hero. The only war in the film was a gentle one, fought between the Kashmiri boatman's idea of a good Indian life—simple traditional living—and the lifestyle of the upper-class "modern" city woman he falls in love with. Having watched with misery as the woman he loves dances with any man who asks her, he provides a moral via his contribution to party music: I feel like a foreigner here, he sings. And: *kaise bhuul jaaun ki main huun Hindustani?* How can I forget that I am Indian? This upholder of the great Indian way was also conveniently turned Hindu by the film—though most boatmen in Kashmir are Muslim. In fact, religion was barely a presence.

Later films from Bombay would make up for this. By the nineties, even Bombay's dreams of Kashmir had grown up and become "real." There was cinematic acknowledgment that things were not quite "normal" in Kashmir Valley. The silly dreams were gone, but not the blinkers. Films like *Roja* (1992), *Mission Kashmir* (2000), and *Yahaan* (2005), looked at reality with a vengeance. But to look at this reality, believe it was fully real, you needed a made-in-India "patriotism." Protest, dissent, Islam, Islamism, terrorism, religion, separatism, nationalisms, the Indian republic, Pakistan and its designs—all could then collapse into one crazy remix. It helped if you believed that Kashmiris are innocent or angry puppets in the hands of the Islamic warmongers from next door. It helped if you equated the fate of the Indian republic with the high-pitched scene in *Roja* when the cryptographer-hero, kidnapped by terrorists, rolls on the Indian flag they set alight. With his body he defends the cloth that is supposed to hold all of India in its warp and weft.

2011: A DESOLATION CALLED PEACE

In real life, in the bits of Kashmir I saw in 2011, and from the disparate voices I heard, it was not a film but two lines of poetry that beat a contrapuntal tattoo in my head. I heard the words of Kashmir's own saint-poet, Lalla Ded, but with a meaning quite different from what she intended: Life here is but an empty breath.[1] And I heard Lalla Ded's descendant in our times, Agha Shahid Ali, every word meaning what he intended: "I am being rowed through Paradise on a river of Hell."[2]

But if the extended family of security forces, the Indian government, the Pakistani government, the varieties of militants, and the venal local politicians had helped make these lines true, the people in the valley, even children with nothing but stones in their hands, seemed more than ready to take back their lives, breathe something hard and strong of their own into them.

I was in Kashmir as part of a small "civil society" delegation. Our visit was intended as a modest step toward building awareness across India on the urgent need to resolve the crisis in Kashmir. In the profusion of testimonies, demands, challenges, solutions and half-solutions heard over the next few days, three motifs recurred. One was overwhelming anger, and fear and hatred of the uniformed guardian viewed as occupier, predator—whether personified by the Kashmir police and their Criminal Investigation Department (CID), the Indian Border Security Force (BSF), the Indian Central Reserve Police Force (CRPF), or the Special Operations Group (SOG). The second motif was a strong sense of who India was to Kashmir, and who it was not—and India here was an unhappy mix of the army, the central and state governments, the law, and the media, particularly television. The third was the sense that the civilian energy of the year before, expressed on the streets with flying stones, marches, and slogans in the summer of 2010, still lay simmering underneath every conversation and encounter.

* * *

The room was lined with photographs of shaheeds—martyrs. All of them were lawyers. I looked at the one right across from me: he had a full head of hair and thick dark eyebrows; the look on his face made him seem older than he must have been. The man, in his forties, was Jalil Andrabi, a well-known human-rights lawyer. I was told he also believed in independence for Kashmir; he was associated with the Jammu and Kashmir Liberation Front (JKLF). In 1996, he was arrested by Major Avtar Singh of the 35th Rashtriya Rifles unit of the army; the major was, for some reason, known as Bulbul—the nightingale. Three weeks into abduction by the nightingale, Andrabi's decomposed body was found floating in the Jhelum River. He had been shot in the head, I was told, and his eyes gouged out. In response to the direction of the high court to arrest Avtar Singh, the Indian government said it did not know where the major was. Besides, the major was no longer employed by the army; and he had not committed the "offense" in his "official capacity." The army then could hardly be held responsible for his actions. Avtar Singh is reportedly living in California, a free nightingale.

We were at a meeting at the Jammu and Kashmir High Court Bar Association at the Saddar court complex. As in Palestine, there seemed to be an astonishing number of the middle class who train to be lawyers in Kashmir. It's as if there is a hope against hope that the law will set right the crimes of occupation in one case, militarization in the other.

But it was not hope I picked up in the room when people began to speak.

"We don't need your healing touch," one man said bluntly. Then I got a taste of the words that would punctuate all accounts: "*your* people."

The anger and frustration in this room had a specific edge: these were lawyers, and how must they see themselves if the law itself had gone awry? It is hard to imagine any lawyer applying the word *legal* to the workings of the Public Safety Act—a law that allows "administrative" and "preventive" detention without a specific charge or a trial. The Bar Association's own president, Mian Abdul Qayoom, and its general secretary, Ghulam Nabi Shaheen, were among those who had been detained. Mian

Qayoom was detained for "illegal activities" such as pro-secession protests. Later, the detention order got more elaborate—the charge was sedition and "waging war against the state." Ghulam Nabi Shaheen was detained for similar charges, and for organizing protests against the detention of Mian Qayoom.

This is the point that was being driven home to us: the members of the Bar Association are taking on matters involving the violation of basic rights—cases of "enforced disappearances," for example. And intimidating lawyers, or punishing them with detention on vague charges, or charges of political protest, is a way to keep them in line.

The lawyers said to us: "As many as 99.9 percent of detention cases are quashed, but still, anyone can be suspected and detained. With laws like this, anybody can be killed anytime, anywhere." Independent reports bore this out: in 2010, for instance, Amnesty International estimated that over two decades, between eight and twenty thousand Kashmiris had been detained under the PSA.

More than one lawyer in the room said to us, "Please educate the people of India about us." This was the education we were to take back, the hard lessons, the unbending syllabus: "Our rights are being violated day after day. Our leadership is not allowed to interact with people. They use the excuse that a house is being used for terrorist operations and the house is destroyed. We are losing lives. We have lost nearly a whole generation. If you push us to the wall, what will our boys do?"

There was bitterness whenever democracy came up in the conversation—the word was constantly coupled with *Delhi*.

"The high court is disabled, the judiciary is not working, the local press is gagged." As for that great romantic image of Indian democracy, the election: no one took seriously elections "facilitated" by men in khaki and green, elections that require a good number of people to be kept out of the way in jail. And those who talk of "human rights" and "development" as if these live in a vacuum—they, we were told, miss the real, *political* point. Democracy cannot be curfewed democracy. One lawyer summed it up: "Democracy and freedom mean choices. What choice do we have?"

* * *

The next morning was gloomy. Though it was April, the overcast sky hung heavy with wintry foreboding. We were driving to Kupwara, north of Srinagar, and, unfortunately for the people living there, close to the Line of Control between India and Pakistan. Parts of Kupwara are famous for the beautiful meadows and fresh air. It was also in Kupwara, in a township called Machil, that three young men, Muhammad Shaif Lone, Shehzad Ahmed, and Riyaz Ahmed, were killed in April 2010. They were supposed to be "infiltrators"; terrorists from across the border. It turned out the "encounter" was staged to collect the reward for killing infiltrators. The three young men singled out to play terrorists had been lured with the promise of jobs.

We saw something of the famous Kashmiri hospitality during our day in Kupwara; but always, sorrow lay like a skin over friendly words and gestures. Living for decades in the midst of infiltration from across the border, different brands of militancy, and most of all, counter-operations by the army, has taken all the fabled fresh air out of the place.

The town hall in Kupwara was full. A man got up with the air of making a formal statement. "Kashmir is an international issue. It should be resolved with UN resolutions." Another man jumped up from the last row of the hall, disrupting the seminar feeling before it took hold of the room. "No compromise," he said clearly. "*Yeh mera watan hai, yeh mera mulk hai*—we will not go back from our demand for independence." His friend, who had been nodding approvingly, added, "If you can't prevail on the powers that be, don't come here and talk to our civil society."

There was a pause. As if to soften the angry moment, a man with a beautiful long face and a colorful sweater stood up. "We didn't chase away the Hindus. Jagmohan did. We will welcome them back." He smiled, as if ready for that homecoming this instant.

(I had heard, the day before, one brave variation of this painful chapter in Kashmir's recent history, the exodus of as many as one hundred thousand Hindus in the years following 1989. Amit Wanchoo, a Kashmiri Pandit trained as a doctor, told us how his family chose to remain in the valley—even after his activist grandfather was killed by militants. "That one decision, not to migrate, and the huge support of my Kashmiri friends, ensured I didn't get to be anti-Muslim.")

In the Kupwara town hall, the next speaker was a tall man in a blue jacket. "We wish Hindustan well," he said, "but..." He spoke softly and reasonably; I could imagine him persuading people though he seemed to have rehearsed what he was going to say. "I want to stay with Hindustan. But if Hindustan does not have space for Arundhati Roy, what place do I have? If Hindustan does not have space for Muslims, what place do I have?"

No one picked up the Muslim thread. I couldn't help being heartened by this, though I knew that the Kashmir I saw had changed in ways not always visible. The old Kashmir, hospitable to a range of ideas and beliefs, a confluence of meeting rivers, had been pushed into the past. The great game of mapping had drawn new borders and boundaries. Along the way, Kashmir's inclusive Islam had been dented by conservative versions, both imported and home-grown.

Now that the necessary gestures had been made, we got down to business. Some of the people in the town hall, maybe many of them, must have talked to delegations before. But still they were not done with what they had to say. There was desperation to be heard; everyone wanted to speak.

"Four of our children were killed by the army." (Cries of *Shame! Shame!* filled the hall).

"Sixty women were raped close by."

"A woman gave birth to a baby with a broken arm."

More eyewitness stories followed, the sort that cannot be politely wrapped up in the impersonal phrase "human-rights violations."

"The government of India and the government of Jammu and Kashmir have no faith in their own judicial system. They are not governed by rule of law themselves. We live in a very big jail, a jail run with sticks and guns. A *danda-raj*."

"Politics is something we have learned through suffering. We have nothing left to lose."

A bespectacled man wearing a beret asked us sharply: "What does *security forces* mean? Does it mean the killing of children?"

It was almost a relief when the *sang-lazan*, the stone-pelters, got their turn to speak.

The boy stood with his feet planted firmly on the ground. "I am Dar Rashid, stone-pelter," he told us. He described what it is like to be tear-gassed. He spoke of his mother and sister, their sufferings. "I can't even cross the road," he said, "without being stopped by an army convoy, or being asked who I am. That's why I throw stones. I am a stone-pelter."

The next stone-pelter, Muzaffar, was not young or a student; he was a schoolteacher. "I lost my job because of an FIR," he said. (By now, we had heard of so many First Information Reports with the police that an FIR was like a compulsory entry on a CV.)

Another teacher said he was also a school principal; he added, with some pride, "Why does a principal start pelting stones?" He answered the question himself: "I can't sit with my hands bound." He took a deep breath then burst out, "I want my Kashmir free."

* * *

Free. And like a mirror image that distorts words, *pushing us to the wall. Danda-raj.* We heard different words that told us this same thing: they were living in a situation, and with the constant feeling, that they had no choices, they were not free. Certainly the Kashmiris I met did not think they had a share in Indian democracy, such as it is. And after the peak reached by popular protest in 2010, the cry for *azaadi* was only growing louder, more firm. This cry of azaadi that has come to live in Kashmir: the word is spoken with passion, or bitterness, or longing. There are many prisms through which freedom is seen, not, perhaps, unlike the ways in which Indians see their ideas of India. In the roundtables I attended, and the breakfast meetings with leaders of assorted groups, I heard much talk of roadmaps. But it is the prospect of freedom that seemed to hold together all kinds of people, all kinds of ideas about how they want Kashmiris to live.

If the idea of freedom is fleshed out in many ways, there seemed to be no doubt about what it is that makes them *not free*. "The substantive content of azaadi cannot be very easily described, but the absence of freedom is a very visible reality in Kashmir."[3]

Perhaps it was easier to pull out evidence of absence than to construct what you may want to put in its place. Absence of freedom: the knock on the door and the armed intruder; closures, curfews, cross fire, rigged elections, burned houses, "enforced disappearances," torture, unmarked graves, widows and half-widows, the missing and the dead.

Even when shots are not being fired, when the streets are open and people carry out their daily business, the memory of yesterday weighs heavily on them, and the fear of tomorrow takes root. Even on a quiet day, the absence of freedom is a desolate peace.

Such desolation has no one cause, and the militants, "theirs" and sometimes "ours," have been part of its complicated history. But over the last decade or more, particularly with anger and sorrow congealing in the hearts of people in 2010, it is India—or, more immediately and tangibly, the instruments of India. Whether from lawyers, journalists, schoolteachers, stone-pelting boys, housewives, or the hard-nosed leaders of various parties and factions, we heard about the mistrust, fear and anger evoked by the "security" forces. There was the apprehension about the increasing amount of land hired or requisitioned by the armed forces. The government is cagey about figures, but estimates have been that that there was one soldier for every fifteen or twenty people. In 2010, there were five hundred thousand armed troops, three hundred thousand army men, seventy thousand Rashtriya Rifle soldiers, one hundred thirty thousand central police forces for a population of one crore.[4] Not surprisingly, a generation of Kashmiris has grown up with soldiers at every street corner, and "often even in their living rooms." The presence of such large numbers of troops—and what they could do and what they have actually done to ordinary Kashmiris—meant that it was getting harder all the time to separate the call for freedom from the call to demilitarize one of the most militarized places in the world.

* * *

These soldiers, instruments of militarization: the ordinary Indian soldier, like ordinary soldiers elsewhere, is far from home, in a place and situation he does not understand. He is poor. Whatever personal humane qualities he may bring with him to Kashmir sinks into the only certainty available in his new surroundings—loyalty to the force.

Men who follow orders, use order, have their brotherhood, their uniforms and guns; but they also need laws. Over and over again, we heard about the "black laws"—the Enemy Agents Ordinance Act (EOA), the Public Safety Act (PSA), and the

Armed Forces Special Powers Act (AFSPA)—and not just from the lawyers' fraternity. PSA and AFSPA have become part of the language spawned by a military siege. Words like "encounter" and "enforced disappearance" are as commonplace as hello and goodbye. We heard about the ways in which this language and these "draconian" laws can mark the lives of people at any time.

PSA can mean prison or house arrest without charge or trial. It may be arbitrary; it may be used only to punish the expression of political views. In other words, PSA helps keep anyone—militant, perceived troublemaker or ordinary citizen—"out of circulation."

AFSPA, the Armed Forces Special Powers Act in force in Kashmir (and the North-East), defines a disturbed area. If the governor of the state or the central government considers the area disturbed or dangerous, and thinks the armed forces are needed to maintain civil law and order, the place can be declared a "disturbed area." The special powers the title of the Act refers to: firing "to the extent of causing death" if public order demands it; the use of force against those who assemble in groups of five or more, or carry weapons, or things capable of being weapons; destroying any place which may have weapons, from which armed attacks may be made, or which may be used as a hideout or training camp for armed volunteers, gangs, and "absconders"; entering and searching any premises without a warrant for people, arms, explosive substances, or stolen property; and arresting, again without a warrant, and with any force required, "offenders."

In other words, AFSPA lets the armed forces search, arrest, detain, and even shoot any Kashmiri with the claim that they are suppressing an armed insurgency.

So while azaadi is, no doubt, "freedom from India" for many, there are other meanings, all of them urgent.

"Aazadi is freedom from fear and insecurity, the humiliations and atrocities the armed forces heap on us."

"Aazadi is, first, freedom from the *fauj*, every kind of security force."

"They can kill a Kashmiri without being held accountable. In fact, a dog's life is more precious than a human being in Kashmir right now! Thus the first azaadi would be the restoration of the right to life."

They were talking of the first freedom, the freedom to live, and to live without fear. Without this first freedom, they would never know when and how they would have to submit to someone who had power over them; or when they would be subject to his violence.

* * *

This is the kind of life that requires a dose of black humor to help you cope. Kashmir has a traditional theatrical form called Bhand Pather. The *bhands* travel from place to place entertaining people with sharp political satire. Or they used to; then criticizing the Indian state (or the militants) became risky. It became safer to laugh at the autocratic raja who ruled before 1947. One of the risky contemporary scripts: A Kashmiri walking down the road is stopped by an army officer. The officer asks the man in Hindi: "Gun kahan rakha hai?" *Where have you kept your gun?* Like many Kashmiris, the man has trouble with Hindi. Also, he has an uncle called Gani whom he calls Gun-e-Kak, a popular

Kashmiri nickname. So he tells the officer in Kashmiri: "Haan, Gun-e-Kak garas manz hai." *Yes, Gun-e-Kak is at home.* Of course the officer thinks he has just heard a confession about a gun hidden in the man's house and begins to beat him.[5]

I wonder what satirical gem the bhands would have made out of the day I met, one after the other, separatist leader Syed Ali Geelani, and Core Commander 15 Corps General Hasnain.

Four of us were driven in a jeep to meet Geelani. Along the way, the jeep swerved off the road, came to a halt. The driver got off, and another man, a passerby, got in. He drove us to a place with a long wall with blue doors at regular intervals. The soldiers or the police—men with guns, at any rate—were waiting to stop us at these doors. We got off the jeep. One of our group, an intrepid journalist nothing seemed to faze, made calls, demanding to know if Geelani was under house arrest, and if he wasn't, why we couldn't met him. While we were hanging around, waiting for the unseen higher-ups to make up their minds, I looked around. It was an ugly little alley the wall made; I tried to imagine what we would see if one of the doors opened; it would be, I thought, a congested neighborhood, small rooms in small houses, one on top of the other.

The call came through and one door opened. Going through the door was like turning into Alice and going down the rabbit hole. The wall with doors turned out to be a stage prop. Behind it lay a beautiful stretch of green grass leading up to a generous-sized house. Inside, we sat on soft carpets, resisting the temptation to lean against the cushions, because we were drinking tea with the "patriarch of separatism," a very thin and very stern man whose woolen cap and white beard made a long face seem longer.

Geelani, I had heard, was pro-Pakistan, but, of course, he spoke to us of India, not Pakistan. "Your work is in Delhi, in India," he told us. Men came and went into the room as Geelani spoke. "Work to remove the stereotypes Indians have about Kashmiris. Kashmiris can't be dubbed terrorists. Their struggle is just and righteous. It's the Indian forces that have unleashed a war of terror against the Kashmiris." As if the word *righteous* prompted him to shift to holy ground, Geelani raised an admonishing finger and recalled Mohammad's last sermon for us: the sanctity of life, the sanctity of the pledged word, the necessity for living in conditions of justice and equality.

Directly from Geelani's house behind the wall, two of us went to meet another Syed, another "Kashmir veteran," though on the "other side"—Kashmir's "senior-most serving Army General," Syed Ata Hasnain.

The other side certainly looked different. It was like straying into a memory of what Kashmir was like before trouble came to it, except this was a domesticated memory. Everything seemed pruned, manicured, and in order in Badami Bagh, corps headquarters of the Indian army. Even the trees and bushes seemed to know which way to grow, when to bloom flowers or shed leaves. But there was time only for a quick impression before we were ushered into a wooden building that used to be a royal hunting lodge. Heels clicked, salutes were made, and we were left with the general in his room.

The general first came to the valley in 1997 as a colonel. He was in charge of "anti-terror operations" and "development activities." The general now spoke to us, in a quiet reasonable tone, of the need to engage with just about everyone, elders, youth, women, businessmen, clerics, academics, hardliners. His approach, he said, was humane. He spoke of the healing touch for the people; of sensitization for the men in uniform.

All this sounded reassuring. It didn't take long, once outside the regimented garden of headquarters, for the comforting bubble to burst.

Later I read the write-up the general sent us. It described the "theme" he had chosen to carry out his most recent mission in Kashmir: "The theme I have adopted after much deliberation and in light of my past field experiences in the Valley, is of employing 'The Heart as MY Weapon'... We need to understand the Kashmiri psyche with sympathy and with love and caring and the heart is the best medium to reach out to the *awaam* even as we carry out the operational part of our charter of reducing if not altogether eliminating terrorism in the Valley."

Another man whose poetry knew how to use the heart as a weapon wrote of his Kashmir: "Your history gets in the way of my memory." And, wrote Agha Shahid Ali, "My memory keeps getting in the way of your history."[6]

THE PLACES KASHMIRI WOMEN LIVE IN: 2012

A year after my visit to Kashmir, there were eleven Kashmiri women round the table in the cozy room lit by the Delhi winter sun. They were there to tell us of their lives. A few of the Kashmiri women spoke of childhood memories; others of crippling fears. All of them spoke of the loss of, and the longing for, a half-forgotten thing called "normalcy."

What is normalcy in Kashmir, what is normalcy anywhere? Like freedom, normalcy is more easily met in the form of its absence.

The question made me recall what a boy I met in Srinagar told me. His grandfather was a retired judge, and highly respected. But this did not protect him from being a Kashmiri, a local who can be suspected of anything. He was stopped by a soldier on the streets, asked to identify himself; the demand was accompanied by a casual slap. The boy's face reddened as he spoke to me, as if he could still feel his grandfather's humiliation. From amid the accounts of arrests, torture, firing, and custodial deaths I had heard, this is what suddenly floated up to the surface. Normalcy means normal relationships—of respect and affection you are not constrained from expressing.

Like people anywhere in the world, Kashmiris want a life in which the little businesses of life become the real business of life—say bringing up children without fear for their physical safety, and with commonplace hopes for their future. Like people anywhere in the world, Kashmiris want a life in which they can enjoy the sunshine and rain in peace.

The women in the room were telling us about the odds against their living such a life, a life with a present and a future. They told us about deaths and disappearances, curfews and closures. Most of all, they told us about plain free-floating fear: worrying if the husband or son who leaves the house will be picked up on suspicion; worrying if the child who goes to school or tuition or to a friend's will return home unharmed. This is a life that has to be lived every day with named and unnamed fears.

But all the women, without exception, also spoke, in one way or the other, about their battles against these odds. About their anger and frustration; their protests; their plans of action; their travel in search of support. They had made the language of resistance their mother tongue.

* * *

The women were gathered in the room to speak about the "situation" in Kashmir. The Delhi women in the room were representatives of Indian civil society in general, and Indian women's organizations in particular. Since the Jammu and Kashmir government has failed to collect even basic data, we had before us data from various independent sources, national and international. Much of this information just about touched the tip of the iceberg; but it was bad enough as it was.

Above all, there was—there is—sexual violence. As always, the women bear the brunt of prolonged armed conflict; of crackdowns, cordon and search operations, and all kinds of "security checks." Rape is the preeminent instrument of punishment, intimidation, coercion, and humiliation, and it is used freely. Rape brings "collective dishonor"—raping their women is seen as a way to punish the men. Just one instance: on the night of February 23, 1991, soldiers of the fourth Rajputana Rifles swooped down on a small village called Kunan Poshpora for a "search operation." The men were taken away for interrogation; the women, as many as thirty women, were raped. (Three years later, when a women's group went to the village, they found that the married raped women had been deserted by their husbands; a seventy-year-old woman who was raped had been thrown out by her son. The young women, whether they were raped or not, had remained single.[7])

Bringing the rapist to book is practically impossible. To begin with, the police are reluctant to register FIRs against members of the troops. And if the FIRs can be filed, sometimes the rape survivor has to file a report to exactly those authorities who have raped her.

The talk turned to missing persons, to the ghostly population of missing and disappeared men who have filled the landscape over the years. These men may be alive and in custody, they may be in one of the numerous unmarked graves. *Enforced disappearances. Half-widows.* Strange new terms become current when harassment and violence become routine. Thousands of people, many of them married men, have been "subject to enforced disappearance by state agencies." In other words, they have been picked up by the troops. In the absence of information about them, the disappeared men's wives become half-widows. Half-widows bear extra suffering: they are left without entitlement to land, homes, inheritance, pensions, or social assistance. They face the constant threat of destitution. And, of course, they are more vulnerable to harassment by the troops.

So frayed is the social fabric that every form of suffering, from rape to the insecurity of daily life, only strengthens social surveillance and policing. Their "own side" takes refuge in patriarchal certainties about controlling women, or in one of the more recent versions of Islam that has crept in to challenge the old syncretic Sufi tradition of Kashmir. Groups such as the Allah Tigers and Lashkar-e-Jabbar insist on women wearing the burqa in public; other militant groups have issued diktats against contraceptives.

Psychiatric disorders thrive in such a climate. Trauma and wounds are not always visible. In the post-1989 years, there has been a sharp increase in mental illness among women—from sleeping disorders to depression to post-traumatic stress disorder (PSTD). The lone psychiatric hospital in the valley is in Srinagar. In 1989, about one thousand seven hundred patients visited this hospital; by 2003, the number had gone up to forty-eight thousand. It does not take an expert to visualize which way the numbers go between 2003 and 2012. And these numbers account for one single hospital in one single city, and for women who are lucky enough to make it to a hospital at all.

* * *

But data does not have a human face. Nor does it have a voice that rises in anger and breaks with sadness. The women around the table, talking to us in Delhi, did.

There was Parveena, who could have been anyone's ordinary but beloved mother. But Parveena is far from ordinary. Her second son, Javaid, was picked up for interrogation by the security forces during a raid in 1990; she has heard nothing of him since. She described her missing son: "He had a stammer," she said. "Maybe that is why he was blessed, he was always cheerful and affectionate. He used to help me cook and wash clothes, and he would study, too. He was not the kind of boy who would ever pick up a gun."

Worry and grief did not stun Parveena into acceptance. Though she had never done anything outside the house alone before, she began an endless round of chasing the police, government, and security officials. In 1994, she set up the APDP, the Association of Parents of Disappeared Persons. She went wherever she could to tell her story and the stories of other parents. She learned to speak for all of them when she asked, "Where are our children? Where is our justice for them?" For twenty-two years, she had been leading protests in a park every month. She would not stop her work, she told us, till all the missing children got justice.

Search for our children! This full-throated cry must have been heard by many people other than us; it must have haunted the people she spoke to day after day, week after week, in demonstrations and sit-ins and meetings in and outside Kashmir. But to date, the association has not been able to recover a single one of their missing children.

Parveena suddenly crumbled before us. All we could do was offer her a glass of water and an embrace. "I can't sleep at night," she told us in a voice that showed the grief behind the strength, "I can't rest. Every time I hear a knock on the door, I think my son has come back."

Then there was Lebul Nisa, a young woman whose maroon headscarf framed her pale moonlike face. She looked delicate but her voice was calm, strong, and mature beyond her years. She is a human-rights lawyer who has worked with half-widows. Up to seven years, she told us, the missing husband is not officially dead. His half-widow could not remarry; she could not lay claim to property. Most likely she had not been educated enough to support herself or her children; she had trouble with shelter, with childrearing, with anxiety and depression. "How do we help half-widows survive?" asked Lebul Nisa.

Half-widows, full widows. We heard of Lebul Nisa's visit to Dardpora Village. Ironically apposite, this cruel name: the place of pain. Close to the Line of Control, Dardpora in Kupwara epitomizes what happens to a place when regular skirmishes over two decades make conflict a way of life. The little village has come to be called the village of widows—the pain in Dardpora personified by the lives the widows have had to lead. One woman took to begging so her daughter could survive; another was heartbroken that she could not pay for a shroud for her dead husband. Still another—who got no "compensation" because her dead husband was described as a militant—had to support four sons on a salary of Rs 650.

Lebul Nisa told us a particularly painful story of a seventy-two-year-old woman who was raped. The security forces told the woman: "If you tell stories to the media, we will send you to heaven even before they have shown their film." It was not surprising, then, that when Lebul Nisa referred briefly to her own life, she said: "Ours is a generation that does not know what a picnic means. It is only a word for us."

We heard other young voices, more edgy than Lebul Nisa's.

Inshah, a researcher and activist, alternated between impatience with the rest of the world and passion for azaadi. She recalled growing up amid homes and schools torn apart by bombs; she recalled the terrible and constant anxiety about the safety of loved ones. *I am a victim, I am a fighter*, she said firmly, ready to take on anyone who disagreed.

As if to balance the picture—or complicate it, as it must be—we heard a Kashmiri Pandit who had to leave the valley. Renu, a teacher, talked poignantly of the Kashmiri Pandits' right to return. "Our suffering should also be counted," she pleaded. "We want to return without having to support any faction." No one in the room contested her right to return home, though there was a digression. Suddenly we were in the middle of a discussion about the Amarnath Yatra. We got a sharp whiff of the way this pilgrimage has been used to try and turn Kashmir into a Muslim–Hindu contest. But even before we could pin down what was being said, the Valley as it is took over again.

We heard Tehmeena, a gentle-voiced doctor who did not speak "politics." She spoke about the women patients who come to her, many of them victims of a range of mental disorders, from depression and anxiety to delusions and hallucinations. For many of them, "new" diseases have taken over their days and nights: sleeplessness or too much sleep, nightmares, low or high blood pressure, palpitations, dizziness or a "falling feeling," twitching hands and facial tics, silence or talking too much, sensitivity to noise, fear of the dark, fear of being alone, a sinking feeling or a heavy feeling in the chest. The list went on; it is amazing what the body is capable of taking on to mirror what the mind is going through.

The more experienced activists in the room hastened to stretch what Tehmeena was telling us to fit a larger context.

Anjum, a columnist and an author, and Hameeda, a university teacher, asked us: What does "militarization" really mean? Anjum and Hameeda then answered the question themselves. It meant the security forces, and sections of the Kashmiri military and police, were growing more brutal by the day. It meant that Kashmir and Kashmiris were subject to the "militarization of place, body, and mind." If this did not change, no other change was possible.

As these women spoke, two language registers sat uncomfortably beside each other. For our benefit perhaps, the women referred to the *security forces*. But we were meant to hear *occupying forces* when Anjum asked us dryly, "Where is the *security*?"

In turn one of the Delhi women asked Anjum about the place women have earned themselves in resistance movements. Had the struggle for azaadi given women a political voice independent of their lives as wives, mothers and sisters?

This was not a popular question; understandable, perhaps, since the women, like women in similar situations elsewhere, wanted to support their men who were being emasculated by the military. Unity was important, and sisterhood went only so far when it was "us" talking to "them." Besides, no one could deny that women had been in the forefront of protest on the streets, especially in the summer of 2010; an image or two of stone-pelting middle-aged women had made its way even to Delhi.

The room fell silent. It was time to sum up, end with that familiar discussion on how public opinion could be mobilized. How the one-sided perception of Kashmir as a land of terrorists could be made more complex, more real, more true.

Even as the women round the table resigned themselves to suggestions, recommendations, petitions, it felt like time was running out. As we left the room, it felt like the Kashmiri women were still waiting for us to speak, or do *something*, even if it was only to respond to a poet's appeal: "Each night put Kashmir in your dreams." Not a fantasy-Kashmir, but a real, suffering, angry Kashmir, a home no longer a home, or a home replaced by a pretend home for all those who have had to leave, Pandit, Sikh, or Muslim.

There is a story in Kashmir about a bird called the shraz. It is in love with the moon. How can you not embrace what you love? The shraz goes up the mountain, as close to the sky as it can. The moon does look closer from this snowy height. The shraz leaps, it flies toward the moon. The moon remains in the sky; the bird falls to the ground and dies. But out of its ashes is born another shraz.

Kashmir harbors this shraz in the real world, where fires are lit on streets and in hearts. Maybe this phoenix will stoke that hope of going home, going home alone, refusing all companions, armed or unarmed, from this side of the border or that. A home that becomes home again: this is what Kashmir, India, and Pakistan owe the boys I met in Srinagar and Kupwara, and the women I met in Delhi.

5

SPEAKING IN HAIKU

1970–1974: JAPAN IN BOMBAY

I was sixteen when I first went to Japan in 1970. I had just finished high school in Manila, where my parents then lived. My sister, brother, and I were in ecstasy because we had been told we were going to Expo 70 in Osaka. Once in Japan, we did everything required of us: gasped at the sight of Mt. Fuji from our plane; politely swallowed the strange acid of the green tea we were served with mind-numbing solemnity; laughed with frank enjoyment as we took the bullet train or fed the deer in Nara; and tried very hard not to fall asleep at the Noh play we were taken to see. We went back to Manila with the mandatory photographs and souvenirs and sightseeing memories.

My first real trip to Japan took place almost two years later, in an island-city far from the Japan Sea.

I was almost eighteen when I left Manila and the family home to explore the big bad world. Taking on the big bad world meant going back to India, Bombay in particular, and growing up by myself. An almost eighteen-year-old in the Bombay of the early seventies could learn many things, and I suppose I did, too. Among the more respectable and acceptable learnings was the reading and writing of poetry, specifically haiku.

There is something irresistible about the small and the powerful. In literature, perhaps the best example of this potent combination is the Japanese haiku. The haiku uses a few words, three or four lines, to hint at a large, mysterious universe. I still recall the sharp intake of breath that accompanied my first reading of Bashō's haiku. To be able to get across so much in just seventeen syllables! I read the famous haiku about the old pond, translated by R.H. Blyth:

> *The old pond*
> *A frog jumps in*
> *the sound of water.*[1]

And the one translated by Lucien Stryck:

> *Summer grasses*
> *all that remains*
> *of soldiers' dreams.*[2]

Like many before me, it was the haiku's power of suggestion I fell in love with. This power has its source in the haiku's use of images, from nature for example. The images mate the incongruous or unlikely pair; I discovered that the classical haiku typically fuses motion and stillness.

Its impressionist nature, its ambiguity, and its ability to reduce a large untidy world into a small space: this is what makes the haiku such an effective little weapon to decode the world. For young people wanting to make sense of what they see and feel, poetry is, in any case, a good way to make "notes for the self." And since haiku allows this to be done in shorthand that challenges both poet and reader, it was—at least when and where I was growing up—something of a rite of passage for young scribblers.

As a teenager trying to become an adult in Bombay, I, too, tried to describe the world around me and within me in telegraphic form. I read all the English translated haiku I could lay my hands on, but Bashō remained the Master. Trying to feed my curiosity about who Bashō was, I learned that he was from a low-ranking samurai family, but left home and became a wanderer in search of his fortune. The fortune turned out to be his haiku. I also learned that Bashō deeply approved of the "here and now" principle of haikai, which is what haiku used to be called. He prized spontaneity.

Most important, I discovered Bashō was something of a country cousin of mine. Bashō means banana tree.

In the spring of 1681, in the rustic outskirts of Edo—a place which would, much later, be called Tokyo—a young man planted a banana sapling by the hut of his teacher. The teacher taught him poetry.

The teacher, who lived alone, watched the plant grow into a tree. He liked the fact that the banana leaves were soft and sensitive; that they were, like him, easily torn when the wind blew from the sea. He liked the flowers, which remained small and diffident in a place too cold for them. He imagined they were lonely, knowing they would never bear fruit. Night after night the teacher sat in his hut and listened to the wind whispering among the banana leaves. One night, it rained. The rain leaked through his roof and fell into the basin he placed on the floor. The raindrops played a regular beat as they fell, one after the other. Wind, rain, and banana leaves played their music to the poet. The listening poet wrote:

> *A banana plant in the autumn gale—*
> *I listen to the dripping of rain*
> *Into a basin at night.*[3]

People began to call the place Bashō Hut, the banana tree hut. The poet-teacher was the Master of the Bashō Hut. Soon he became just Bashō—a name he was happy to adopt for the rest of his life.

Unlike the daffodils and violets and dandelions of English poetry, none of which I had seen to date, a banana tree was real. So was a hut named after a banana tree. As for a poet calling himself a banana tree, that was not exactly familiar, but it was a poetic leap that spoke to me. If the daffodil was commonplace elsewhere, the banana was our humble counterpart, and a fit subject for poets. Bashō's name and his poetry assured me that even I, banana-eating Indian though I was, could search for a homegrown voice.

Not long after I discovered the haiku (and perpetrated many of my attempts on tiny sections of the Bombay populace), I discovered another writer who showed me that the unsentimental, calm yet intense soul of haiku need not remain confined to poetry.

Though we did not use the word "postcolonial" like a tic in the seventies, I suppose that's what we were, because the Bombay

University's literary canon then consisted entirely of white males from England. Women in general, and Americans and Russians, were mostly reduced to a few tantalizing footnotes. The rest of the world, including the populous parts we came from, barely existed. But on one of my forays down the hill from Sophia College, I discovered a sensibility that could feed the hunger my postcolonial classroom could not. I found, in a hole-in-the-wall bookshop that should have been given deemed university status, a copy of Yasunari Kawabata's *Snow Country*. I learned then that Bashō's haiku style could stretch over a whole novel.

In the Introduction to his translation of *Snow Country*, Edward G. Seidensticker says, "The haiku manner presents a great challenge to the novelist. The manner is notable for its terseness and austerity, so [the] novel must be like a series of brief flashes in a void." This *is* Kawabata's style: mingling the experiences of all the senses, hinting delicately at the meanings these experiences may lead us toward. The silence of a winter night, for example, may roar in Kawabata's world. The sound of running water may appear round and feel soft. Or, in a quiet and dexterous leap, a bell sounds within the song of the tea kettle, then turns into a woman's feet. Seidensticker points out that Kawabata's literary lineage should rightly be traced back to the seventeenth-century haiku masters.

Simplicity, openness, depth, and lightness: how are these haiku traits used in more spacious forms? *The Sound of the Mountain*, a novel by Kawabata that was made into a Toho film by Mikio Naruse, gave me some answers. Considered by some critics to be Kawabata's best work, *The Sound of the Mountain* uses a series of linked episodes to depict a crisis, or a web of crises, in the Ogata family in Kamakura. The family patriarch, Shingo, is a Tokyo businessman. He is only sixty-two, but he is close to retirement. Perhaps this is one reason he is beginning to suffer brief memory lapses. Or being afflicted with either sleeplessness or strange and disturbing dreams. Or hearing sounds no one else does—such as the sound of the novel's title that wakes him from sleep one night, "like wind, far away, but with a depth like a rumbling of the earth." Most of all, he is suddenly looking at his family with new eyes—his philandering son, his unhappily married daughter, his unimaginative wife, and most of all, his beautiful and heartbreakingly brave daughter-in-law. He is actually *seeing* them, an experience that not only changes them in his eyes, but changes his understanding of his own life. His perception of human relationships shifts subtly but irrevocably.

The scenes of daily family life are interwoven with dreams and memories, but also with images from the natural world. The mountain, the cherry tree in the yard, the birds and insects of a summer evening, two pine trees Shingo sees from the commuter train he takes every day: all these speak to him in a new way on matters of love, desire and aging.

Like so much of Kawabata's work, *The Sound of the Mountain* is written in spare prose akin to poetry—delicate contrapuntal touches and brief scenes to tell a larger story. This comes through even in translation. The film directed by Naruse is faithful to the novel in the attention it pays to texture and perspective. As for using the delicate language of hints, there is the final sequence of the film, set in an extending walkway in a park. Kikuko, the daughter-in-law who has moved Shingo so deeply and made him feel afresh, has a rare emotional outburst as she confesses to having had an abortion. And strangely, both receive a kind of unspoken solace from each other. It's the kind of revelatory moment in a relationship that makes up one of the arresting "haiku images" of the film.

But the best haiku bridge between forms was, perhaps, identified by Kawabata himself. Though known for his many novels, Kawabata also wrote more than a hundred two or three-page stories which he thought expressed the essence of his art. He called these "tanagokoro no shosetsu" or palm-of-the-hand stories, and they are fine examples of the dictum that what is unsaid is as important, if not more important, that what is actually said. "Many writers, in their youth, write poetry," said Kawabata. "I, instead of poetry, write the palm-of-the-hand stories." Three months before his death, Kawabata wrote "Gleanings from Snow Country." This work was actually a miniaturization of *Snow Country*, the novel which had begun as a single short story and brought the writer such acclaim. The bare bones to which Kawabata reduced the novel speak of his lifelong commitment to the haiku, the mode of expression that distils the world down to its essence.

TOKYO AND YAMAGATA, 2003:
TRANSLATING GAIN AND LOSS

Real life has such a hard time learning poetry. In 2003, I went back to Japan for a second visit. This time I was more than grown up. I was part of a "writers' caravan" and we were to talk of our work, of this and that, in Tokyo; then go to Yamagata for a "water festival" where we were to speak, in the best literary manner we could summon, about water.

Tokyo was all official; what I imagine it must feel like when government meets government, except we were writers and no government would have allowed any of us in its corridors. Despite its being choreographed, I was happy to talk and listen; but it had to be done through interpreters. Every day I had to decode what was being said to me, and what others thought I was saying to them, through the losses and gains of translation. I could have sworn the interpreter spoke of S & M into our headphones when we were given the impression we were to listen to a feminist take on literature; and when some of us spoke of the US invasion of Iraq, and Japan's stand on the invasion, we noticed our Japanese counterparts looking at us in utter amazement. Since then I have encountered many creative interpreters who can turn what I say by 360 degrees; but it was in Japan I first learned that an interpreter, or a translator, is *the* heroic figure of our times.

* * *

Tokyo challenged me in many ways, but I could not find my Japan-in-Bombay there. It was in my next stop, Yamagata, where I found a faded ghost of Bashō waiting for me by the water.

There are some places in the world you have already met—in books, in your personal history, maybe in your dreams. It is hard meeting the real thing face to face. There is a character in one of Kawabata's novels, a Tokyo businessman called Shimamura, who considers himself an expert on ballet. He is passionate about ballet, he knows all there is to know about it; but he has never seen a ballet performed. Nor does he want to see the ballet performed by Japanese troupes. He prefers the unique pleasure of being in love with someone he has never seen. I knew what this felt like. When I first went to England in my early twenties, it was hard to look at the England before me—such a small place, too small to contain my made-in-India Chaucer and Shakespeare and Swift and Dickens. Like Shimamura, I wanted, most of all, to shut my eyes, remain in the England I knew so well.

I didn't get a whiff of Edo in Tokyo; so it was in Yamagata where I hoped to meet Bashō. My old friend and hero, Matsuo Bashō, visited Yamagata in 1689. Yamagata Prefecture is in the southwest corner of Tōhoku, facing the Sea of Japan. Yamagata City flourished during the Edo Period (1603–1867) as a castle town and post station; it was also famous for *beni*—red safflower dye used to make handspun silk. Like Bashō, I saw Yamadera, literally Mountain Temple. When Bashō was there, he wrote a famous haiku which Robert Hass translated as

> *Stillness—*
> *the cicada's cry*
> *drills into the rocks*[4]

Long ago, the rocks round Yamadera were considered by some as the boundary between this world and the next. A good place, then, for a temple. Bashō must have considered these rocks and wished he were a cicada so he could drill his way to another life.

The rocks Bashō saw were still there for me to see. But the cicadas would not speak to me. Though I was in Japan, I had to imagine the shrillness of cicadas as if I were in Bombay once more.

Bashō was once a guest in a house where he got a lot of writing done. The place was called the House of Fallen Persimmons. I was not sure if this was in Yamagata, but I was taken to see a house with one of those achingly lovely arranged-yet-spontaneous Japanese gardens. So much sensibility combined with the fresh cold air made me hungry, and I beamed approvingly when a plate of wine-soaked *kaki*—persimmon—was passed around. Politeness can be the hardest wall of all when you have no common language, when you can't say, Oh please, may I have some more? I waited in the circle we had formed on the floor mat, sitting on our knees in Japanese fashion, hoping the plate would be passed around again. It was all taking too long. I moved to the plate, as elegantly as I could manage on my knees, and used the well-worn formula of flattering a host by claiming that second and third helpings were irresistible. The frozen unsmiling faces around me said I had broken some rule of etiquette. Since I was damned anyway, I took the plate round the circle—all on my knees, enough of an act of contrition as far as I was concerned—and offered everyone a piece. I suspect this was not in the rule book either; but there seemed to be an unspoken consensus that I had saved face. A woman took a long white strip of gold-edged cardboard and wrote (or "painted") a poem which she said described me. Two others followed suit. I was later told what the poems were about when the translator caught up with us. But all I could make of it was that the poems, like the garden and the persimmon in wine, looked pleasing. The persimmon poems remain, to this day, a pretty mystery.

When you are, for practical (and impractical) purposes minus a working language, you tend to want some time to yourself, away from the need to speak and listen. Like all Indians, I have been trained to suffer large crowds outside the home, and smaller, equally noisy crowds of friends and family at home. I have also been trained to cope with overwhelming hospitality, Indian style. In Japan, too, they can wear you out with hospitality, especially the kind offered by strangers—the professionals. In Yamagata, I found I could not escape unsolicited kindness for a minute. As I paddled around with a group of women in the hot springs, all of us naked, a woman swam up behind me and scrubbed my back. I could not enter an elevator, or exit one, without much bowing and birdlike voices welcoming me or thanking me for using the elevator, the shop, the hotel, even the loo. When I ran away to be alone by the seashore and came back with seashells in my hand, one of the birds rushed across with a plastic bag for the shells, and led me to the ladies' room so she could wash the sand off my hands. I took refuge in saké, cold, warm, any flavor and quantity. I wondered if Bashō would have needed saké to navigate his way through India.

* * *

While sitting by the sea—this time not gathering shells that would need another plastic bag—I thought of my Bombay in the seventies, and my Japan-in-Bombay of the time; and the real life

Japan I was now looking at through the cloudy windowpane of a language I did not know. The multilingual mess of a Bombay childhood should have prepared me better for the tricks language plays on travelers, both at home and elsewhere. But only now, all these years later, I felt, with full force, the impossibility of living in a world without translation.

Received wisdom has any number of gloomy precepts about the loss of translation: that it is merely an echo; that the best part is lost in translation. In India in particular, given the vexed relationship between English and the other Indian languages, many people like to insist that an English equivalent can never be found for this or that word in Marathi, or Kannada, or Bengali. Happily, there are the imaginative takes on translation as well; not only on its necessity and the wonderful accidents it sometimes leads to; but on the fundamental relationship between original and translation as being somewhat akin to the relationship—shaky but essential—between dream and waking life. The expert on all such convoluted matters, Borges, said the original is unfaithful to the translation. I liked this when I was in Japan. I liked thinking that if I looked through the windowpane of translation, I could see that boundaries were not rigid, that knowledge and idea and beauty did not have a home anywhere in particular, not even the "west." It helped me see the ways in which science and ideas, story and food, traveled to make knowledge and culture at various intersections in India or Egypt or Iraq or the Mediterranean or Greece or Spain.

The petty details of real life travel in our times do not always let us see translation at its most heroic, though. Perhaps we should give up our little word-and-phrase guidebooks, I thought. Perhaps the haiku, with its impressionist exchanges, is the best mode of speech when you need to acknowledge both the happy and unhappy accidents of translation. Then I recalled *Bel Canto*, a novel I had read recently by the American writer Ann Patchett. The novel seemed to belong here, in this moment in the cool gray Japanese evening by the sea.

The story of *Bel Canto* in bald form: a poor unnamed country in South America holds a birthday party for a Japanese company man hoping to improve trade opportunities. Katsumi Hosokawa is the chairman of a large electronics company in Japan. He is also an ardent lover of opera. Though he has never set eyes on Roxanne, an American soprano, he is in love with her voice. Roxanne is invited to perform at the party, and Hosokawa arrives with his translator, Gen Watanabe. The party is at the home of the vice-president of the country. (The president skips the party because it clashes with his favorite soap on TV.) A "terrorist" group, expecting the president to be there, storms the party. They decide to take the guests, or at least the important ones, hostage. All kinds of demands are made; the government cannot meet them; and there is a stand-off—a strange limbo-like time, an almost-utopia, in which anything seems possible, even people talking to each other.

Though a bloody confrontation waits like an inevitable end, there is the time in the house—with people from different places, speaking different languages, learning to speak to each other. Romance stirs despite impediments. Love blooms. The love between Hosokawa and Roxanne can only be called open-ended, since neither speaks the other's language. But languages are learned, including the language of music. Music, it turns out, is the most powerful language of all. The singing voice is able to evoke the most human responses—harmony, compassion, a sense of what really matters, a sense of difference and sameness coexisting in real life.

The most powerful insight of the novel is that for all kinds of people to survive together, the one indispensable person is the translator. Everyone needs him to interpret for them, and Gen Watanabe, a soft-spoken young man usually on the edge of all groups and events, finds himself at the heart of this strange community and the unfolding situation. Without Watanabe, Hosokawa cannot express his love for Roxanne; the young terrorist Carmen cannot learn to read, write, or love; and the others cannot understand life-and-death instructions.

The story is located in a setting increasingly familiar to even the most cushioned people: troubled places; places which can become troubled places when and where you least expect it. Troubled places tend to be multilingual, metaphorically and literally. In a situation when you *have* to understand to survive, or in a situation when you have to be understood and counted as a communicating human, the translator is the hero. With this hero in place, everyone—kidnapper, kidnapped, powerful, powerless, man, woman—grows a voice, grows human. Their stories interleave fear, compassion, hope, progress, learning, change. Disaster is inevitable, but in the interim, every stereotype is overturned. The novel is full of teaching and learning exercises—music lessons, reading lessons, language lessons,

lessons in love, lessons of self-discovery, and discovery of others you would not have encountered at home.

There is more than one way in which language makes a home. We need a Gen Watanabe, loving interpreter, when we travel, whether we travel at home or elsewhere. And we need haiku, since its function, as Bashō once said, "is to rectify common speech."

6

TRAILBLAZING IN ANDALUSIA

CÓRDOBA 2009:
THE HAND OF FATIMA, THE HAND OF MIRIAM

All you have to do is look around you in Córdoba to know the truth: the world is a mixed-up place. The narrow streets, the houses hanging on to them, the tiles and colors and trees, the music, the food, the names of places, language itself—all say they are not just Spanish, or just Arabic-Berber-Islamic-Moorish, or Jewish, or just Roman remains. But as it often happens, the present plays deaf to messages from the past, even when they are loud and clear. The past is a collector's item, a tourist trap; a fly in amber on display. I enjoyed it—no visitor should pretend to be immune to the allure of packaged pasts. But it left me dissatisfied. I wanted more. As I walked through the streets of Córdoba, a suspicion grew in me. To understand the slippery, almost cruel games played between remembering and forgetting, you have to play discoverer in twenty-first-century Andalusia.

My own little journey of discovery began not in the bewildering mosque-cathedral, but northwest of La Mezquita, in the heart of La Judería. I was wandering in the Jewish Quarter, happily lost, when I saw what appeared to be a lovely house at the corner of Calles de los Judíos and Averroës. It turned out to be a fourteenth-century house, now a small museum called Casa de Sefarad. I went in.

I had read a little about the Jewish Quarter, apparently one of the largest in Europe; about the Moorish streets that recall the prosperity of the Jews during the time of Córdoba's caliphate. The Sephardic Jews—Spanish Jews, or, more precisely, Jews of the Spanish rite—were very much part of Córdoba's heady mix till their expulsion from Spain in 1492. But it was around the eleventh and twelfth centuries that the Sephardic Jews flourished commercially and intellectually. This was also Córdoba's time in the global spotlight. In the midst of Dark Ages elsewhere, Córdoba shone like a star in Western Europe. There was prosperity; and for the people, it meant a comfortable life, with paved streets, medicine, science, philosophical debate, poetry, music, and spectacular buildings. Literacy was widespread; the libraries and institutes of learning rivaled those of Baghdad. Everyone used Arabic, but translation flowered and flourished.

The interiors of the Casa de Sefarad fulfilled the promise of the exterior. But I saw more than another beautiful old house. The museum's interests I found refreshingly different; for once the past was not the same old series of mind-numbing acts of aggression or grandeur. Instead, it was about music, poetry, ideas—and in particular as practiced by the women of Andalus.

But it was women's hands that caught my attention first. At the well-stocked museum shop, I saw rows of gold and silver hands. All right palms, all sizes, some encrusted with a glinting stone like an all-seeing eye. Lone open palms, each stiff finger meticulously outlined. I picked up a tiny silver hand to admire it. The three middle fingers were extended and stuck together. The thumb and the little finger curved outward, perfectly symmetrical.

The woman behind the counter told me it was called *mano de Fatima*. The hand of Fatima. It was a good-luck charm, she said, an amulet called *hamsa*. (I was briefly distracted by the fact that where I come from, a *hamsa* is a swan.) It is also, the woman went on, called the hand of Miriam. I chose one of the little silver hands, a hand that could be Fatima's, Miriam's, and now mine, and hung it round my neck. I liked having Fatima and Miriam meet at my throat, sharing, now and then, my voice.

Later I heard more about the hand; not all of it sat well with my fantasy of sisterhood. Stories, like real life, can strip you of the prettier features of illusion.

Fatima, the daughter of the Prophet Muhammad, married Ali, his nephew. She is supposed to have performed many miracles: when she prayed in the desert, for instance, it began to rain. In Anatolia, there is a story about the mano de Fatima. One day Fatima was cooking halvah when the door opened and her husband came home with a new bride. Naturally Fatima was upset. She dropped the wooden spoon she was stirring the halvah with. But she continued to stir. Her hand had become the spoon. She stirred; but she didn't feel her hand scalding, burning. Then her husband came up to her and spoke to her. What are you doing here? he asked, as if he couldn't see. Her hand came back to her; and with it, pain.

So: Fatima's open hand as a symbol of patience, abundance, and faithfulness; and the hope that those who wear the hand will not only be blessed with virtue, but also, in a happy leap of logic, good luck. When the fingers are spread apart, the hand protects you from evil; when they are closed together it brings you good luck. Apparently the hand, the eye, or the number five in Arabic and Berber tradition confront the evil eye—as if they are saying *khamsa fi ainek*—five fingers in your (unfriendly) eye.

The Arabic *khamsa* for five; the Hebrew *hamesh* for five. Fatima and Miriam. The hand of Miriam, sister of Moses and Aaron.

In the Exodus stories of Miriam, she saves her baby brother Moses; she is the prophetess who takes a timbrel in her hand and leads the women in dance, singing of God as they cross the Red Sea. A well follows her as they later cross the desert; the well shadowing Miriam quenches the people's thirst. But when she speaks against her brother Moses' choice of bride, she is punished. She turns a snowy white, described sometimes as leprosy, sometimes as vitiligo. She is healed—at her brother's intercession—and finally dies in the wilderness.

In fact, *al-kaff*, the hand, has been around for a long time and in all kinds of places. The open right hand as a source of protection, blessing: the Hand of the Goddess, the hand of the Buddha, the Hand of Aphrodite, the Hand of Fatima, the hamsa or khamsa, the Hand of Miriam, and the Hand of Mary.

* * *

As I walked around the Casa de Sefarad, I noticed a woman arranging things, completely at home in the elegant old house. She was well built, a woman who looked like she did not give up easily. Her flawless complexion shone with good health. I asked her a few questions. I don't know if it was a particularly lean time of day—there weren't too many people around—or whether it was because she liked my questions. But she spoke to me at length about her family; how they had worked hard at setting up the museum with funds from America.

Then she changed the topic suddenly. "I know what you will want to see," she said. "Come with me." I followed her to an inner room and gasped when I saw the walls. "The famous women of Al Andalus," she said with the gesture of a magician who not only knew what I wanted to see, but could also produce it out of thin air.

There were four women on the walls—on the murals designed and painted by Jose Luis Munoz Luque using graphite, tempera, acrylic, gold leaf, and oil on wood. We began with the old woman to the left. "She is Fatima Bint al-Muthanna," my new friend told me. Fatima was born in Córdoba, though she later moved to Seville. There she devoted herself to teaching. Philosopher, mystic, but also a jurist—it is not surprising that she had great influence over those she taught, including the mystic Ibn Arabi.

But it's the next portrait which held me in thrall—so much so that I unfairly forgot about the remaining two women.

This woman leaned casually against a niche in the wall. Everything about her spoke of confidence. Her face was dreamy but strong; every feature, eyes, nose, chin, well defined. Her uncovered hair was a little unruly—as if some of the curls could not be subdued, or as if she had just got out of bed after reading a book or making love. The lower part of her dress wrapped itself round her legs, outlining their shape, leaving the ankles showing. Round her neck hung a pendant like a piece of mounted writing.

"Who is this," I asked the museum lady.

"This is Wallada," she said. "Wallada the Umayyad."

ANDALUS, CIRCA 11TH CENTURY: THE FAIR LADY'S LITERARY SALON

Wallada bint al-Mustakfi, also known as Wallada the Umayyad, or simply Wallada, lived in Córdoba, sometime between 1001 and 1091. She was the daughter of the Caliph al-Mustakfi Billah, Mohammed the Third, who had no male heir; but still it needed a certain kind of society to ensure that she would inherit her father's wealth. The city, the times, the woman—all needed to be open enough for Wallada to do what she did with her inheritance. She set up a literary hall in Córdoba which attracted leading poets and intellectuals. She used the hall to conduct classes for women in poetry—and the art of love. The women in these classes were a mixed lot. Several were from the nobility, but there were common women as well. Some were slaves bought by Wallada.

Wallada styled herself as the reigning debutante of Córdoba. But she was no garden-variety debutante. She hosted salons for poets, musicians, and artists—men and women—many centuries before France's legendary Madame de Rambouillet held sway over her literary salon. Wallada gathered around her the finest poets and musicians of Al-Andalus. They would sit around her on cushions and rugs, improvising ballads and epic sagas to the sound of the lute and zither. Wallada was herself a poet, writing in Arabic. She was partial to the Córdoban practice of poets competing with each other to finish incomplete poems. Almost all these poets were men, but that didn't deter Wallada. Not only did she take part, but she also, with her quick word and her agile twists of thought, earned herself a reputation for skill.

Most of all, she was a free spirit, choosing to remain unmarried though she had several lovers. And there was a grand passion, too, in her life. It was during one of those complete-the-poem events that she met Ibn Zaydún (or Ibn Zaidoun).

Ibn Zaidoun was a nobleman with considerable political influence, but he had ties with the Banu Yahwar, rivals of Wallada's Umayyad clan. This gave the relationship between Ibn Zaidoun and Wallada a controversial edge, but they managed to conduct a very public love affair. It appears, in fact, that their love story assumed a life of its own, almost overshadowing his political reputation. Ibn Zaidoun was a leading figure in the courts of Córdoba and Seville—even his love poems spoke of his love for the city—but people tended to think of him first as the man who was having a scandalous affair with Princess Wallada.

Only nine of Wallada's poems have survived. Five of these are satirical, even caustic. The best lines were written for the love of her life, Ibn Zaidoun, but they are not all loving. Their affair was a stormy one, and some of her harshest satire was addressed to him. But in the Córdoba of 2009, I saw that this unconventional couple is remembered in a less troublesome fashion—simply as *los enamorados*, the lovers. A sculpted pair of hands stands in El Campo Santo de los Mártires, a plaza near the old medieval walls. The lovers' hands, one of Ibn Zaidoun's, one of Wallada's, do not make it clear if they are already lovers, or just about to embark on their affair. Each hand seems to be straining toward the other. The hands just about touch; it is as if yearning has not yet been fulfilled. The one to the right holds itself sideways, like a call to the other. The other hand has just touched the calling hand; it may clasp it any minute. Both hands are safe, fixed on a commemorative stone engraved with what I was told are two tender love poems in Arabic, with a Spanish translation. The love poems, and the lovers' hands, are shaded by a marble roof-like slab supported by four elegant pillars. But the lovers, Wallada certainly, will be happy to know that the structure is unwalled, open to the world.

These hands and poems feed our need for romance—whether in the present or the past. They make Wallada something of a romantic, being remembered only for her love, for only one love affair. What was she really like, this passionate and daring princess? What would she have thought of being remembered in her city, a city she both loved and challenged, as a tender hand, a devoted lover and beloved? The chances are she would have recited a caustic verse or two.

* * *

Here is Wallada, ready to go out into the streets of Córdoba, on her way to the women in the hall waiting for the lesson of the day. Wallada leaves home with her best student. This protégé, Muhya bint al-Tayyani, daughter of a fig seller, has been living in the palace for a while at the princess' invitation. (Later, after Wallada's death, Muhya would pay tribute to her benefactress with a number of "kind satires.")

For now, Muhya looks at Wallada with admiring eyes, no hint of satire on her lips or in her thoughts. She knows every inch of Wallada's face by heart, but it takes her breath away as if she is seeing the face for the first time. Muhya is not the only one looking at Wallada. As always, all eyes are on her. It is one thing for the city, for the aristocratic opinion-makers, to have an exotic image of ideal beauty. But to see this ideal grown human with flesh and blood, walking proud and tall past you! The curls hanging on either side of her face have a golden sheen to them. Her skin is pale, milky. Her eyes are blue. The city, aristocrats or otherwise, can find no fault in her looks. If she did nothing but display the fair skin and the blue eyes, she would still be admired, so exotic is she. But there is a special quality to Wallada's beauty. She is intelligent; she has a sharp tongue she is ready to use; she is bold.

She is in the streets without a veil. And her tunic is transparent, a fashion she has picked up from the harems of Baghdad. There are verses embroidered on her sleeves, the sort of verses unlikely to pass muster in a harem, in a palace or elsewhere.

Córdoba is liberal enough; perhaps it can't help being liberal, given the crazy mix of cultures, the constant debate among ideas. There are enough people who not only defend her brazen flouting of the veil, an upper-class convention, but also admire the style with which she does it. But there are, as always, the spoilsport mullahs, on the lookout for what they call perverse. They are ready to be harsh, let the world know they are enraged. Besides, it is not the best of times to wear your rebellion like a flaming scarf on your body, especially if you take that body out in the streets. It is the time of the great rebellion, the *fitna*, and the Berbers are rising against the Umayyad Caliphate. Tensions are high.

Wallada and Muhya pass unmolested this time, too. There are more approving glances, more gasps of admiration than looks of disgust. Only Wallada has not taken note of any of this today. Today she is not thinking of the effect she has every time she steps out of her palace. She is not even thinking of what she is going to do with her women pupils in the hall, whether she is going to stun them with a new verse, or the delicious details of a particularly piquant act of love.

She is preoccupied with her own love life this morning.

The salon last night: she goes over it in her mind. She knows she sang well. And she looked good. She had on a new robe, the embroidered words on the sleeves fresh and forthright. On the right sleeve, in a deep forest green mixed with gold, she said: "I am fit for high positions, by God, and go on my way with pride." On the left sleeve, in gold thread interspersed with pink: "I allow my lover to touch my cheek, and bestow my kiss on him who craves it." As usual, two or three of the men lolling on the silk cushions recited poems they made up on the spot, all poems inspired by her song, and her not so secret love for Ibn Zaidoun.

Ibn Zaidoun; her love; their love; the image of last night grows less rosy.

156

Maybe their love is getting too famous. Maybe it is getting to be such a showpiece, it has begun to outshine the lovers themselves. Who doesn't know about that evening when her eyes held his and she said, for everyone to hear, "I fear for you, my beloved. I fear that even this loving gaze of mine, or the ground you tread on, or the hours that pass us, may snatch you away from me. Even if I could hide you in the pupils of my eyes, even if I could hide you there till the Day of Judgment, my fear would not go." And Ibn Zaidoun matched look and word, taking her hand in his. "With the jasmine you offer me, I collect bright stars from the hand of the moon."

But last night there had been no ardent words, only anger.

Last night, her lines had been needle-sharp with scorn: "You know that I am the moon of the skies. But, to my disgrace, you have preferred a dark planet."

She does not want to think about this dark planet now, give it a form, confirm its color, name it as a slave or a woman or a man. She does not want to think it was a person, not a planet, that made her, Princess and poet Wallada, woman who showed her face to the city, a mere part of a humiliating triangle. There are other men in the city; more than enough willing men. There is Ibn Adbus, the wazir, who she can have if she snaps her fingers.

She should be giving her attention to that list, taking stock of what Ibn Abdus had to offer. Instead she composes one riposte after another to Ibn Zaidoun. The more she does this, the more crude she gets. "Your nickname," she thinks, "is Number Six. And it will remain your nickname till you die. Because you are a whoremonger, a bugger, a cuckold, a swine, a thief." She smiles at Muhya, who is surprised at this unprovoked smile that combines anger, spite, and gloating. "A phallus. A penis," thinks Wallada, then goes beyond name-calling. "If a phallus could become a palm tree, you would turn into a woodpecker."

* * *

Ibn Zaidoun didn't do too badly with quarrelsome poetry either. When he saw Ibn Abdus and Wallada walking side by side in the streets of Córdoba, he wrote to her: "You were nothing to me but a sweetmeat. I took a bite of it, then tossed away the crust. That's what the rat is chewing on now." The city was amused; the wazir was not exactly popular, and they liked hearing him described as a rat. But the bitter arrow found its mark. The wazir's complaint to the caliph showed his wazir-like ability. He ignored the rat bit. "What kind of man," he asked the Caliph, "compares the princess to a pastry? Only a dangerous, mutinous poet. Only a traitor."

The Caliph was fond of Ibn Zaidoun. But the court did what courts do: it intrigued. Ibn Zaidoun fell out of favor. He was imprisoned, then exiled. Later, when the Caliph died and Ibn Zaidoun returned, the lovers forgave each other and took up their stormy relationship where they had left off. The passion was still there, but it was different now; Wallada lived in the wazir's house, under his protection. Better to make exile home, thought Ibn Zaidoun, and packed his bags for Seville again. There he would be the favorite poet of the Sultan's court.

In any case the Umayyad universe was crumbling. And Ibn Zaidoun would write his best verse in exile. His *qasidas* were odes equally elegiac about Wallada and the gardens of Córdoba. Or the Madinat al-Zahra, not only lost to him, but ruined in the turbulence that marked the passing of the Umayyads. For Ibn Zaidoun, it was a paradise lost; but it was also a loss that sparked a powerful longing, and powerful poetry. He spoke of the woman he loved, the city he loved, and the times which made such love possible:

> *With passion from this place, al-Zahra,*
> *I remember you.*
> *...A tenderness sweeps me*
> *When I see the silver*
> *Coiling waterways*
> *Like necklaces detached*
> *From throats. Delicious those*
> *Days we spent while fate*
> *Slept. There was peace, I mean,*
> *And us, thieves of pleasure.*
> *Now only flowers*
> *With frost-bent stems I see...*[1]

And Wallada? She lived on to love, sing, write poetry, and remain, we must assume, as independent as she could be. She died, the tale goes, the same day that the Almoravids, the Berbers commonly called *al-mulathimun*, or the veiled ones, entered Córdoba.

GRANADA CIRCA 12TH CENTURY:
WARRIOR POETS HAFSA BINT AND NAZHŪN BINT

I took a bus from Córdoba to Granada. It was hard to let go of the Córdoba of memory, even for a few days. Out of almost eight hundred years of Arab Spain, Córdoba held the place of honor for the first three centuries. By the tenth century, when the princess poet Wallada walked the streets, the city had more than palaces; it had streetlights, hundreds of public baths, well-stocked libraries. It was, simply, the first city of Europe.

But with the caliphate falling apart in Córdoba in the eleventh century, Al Andalus shrank, over the next two hundred years, till all that remained to the Arabs was the kingdom of Granada. Granada reached its peak in the fourteenth and fifteenth centuries.

In the Granada of 2009, this peak was recalled to me by two adjacent hills that rise above the modern lower town and hold the Alhambra and Albaicín. The Alhambra is indescribable, which is why, perhaps, it has been described so often. Albaicín still bears witness to the urban nature of the medieval Moorish settlement. But whether in the Alhambra, or a narrow, sloping lane of the "Arab quarter" museumized in what used to be flourishing Albaicín, the voices I heard were those of Wallada's distant cousins, writing and loving a hundred years after her.

Hafsa bint al-Hajj al-Rakūniyya, more commonly known as Al-Rakūniyya, was born in Granada around 1135 and died in Marrakesh around 1191. Like her Córdoban predecessor Wallada, Hafsa belonged to the upper class—she was the daughter of a

Berber nobleman in Granada and she received a superior education. Again, like Wallada, she was a poet and the lover of a poet, Abu Ja'far Ibn Said; and many of her poems take the form of a dialogue with him. There was no coyness or fear of convention in her expression of love. She takes the initiative for a meeting in a poem she writes to Abu Ja'far:

> *Will you come to me or I to you?*
> *My heart will go where you wish.*
> *You will not thirst if you ask me to come,*
> > *nor will the sun burn you.*
> *My lips are a clear, sweet spring;*
> > *the branches of my hair cast deep shadow...*[2]

Her lover's reply is appreciative of this unusual "visit by the garden to the breeze":

> *If I can find a way, I will go to you.*
> *You are too important to come to me.*
> *The garden does not move, but receives*
> > *the soft puff of the breeze.*[3]

Hafsa is a discriminating receiver of love poems. She is skeptical on one point in Jafar's response—his implication that the garden delighted in the lovers' rendezvous through its scents and sounds. Maybe the garden acts out of envy, she says, not admiration. Another time, Hafsa waits at Jafar's door, hoping to be let in. Of this moment, she writes:

To you has come a visitor with a gazelle's neck
With the black night of her hair that
    shows off the rising crescent moon,
With eyes that hold the magic of Babylon,
    a tongue better than wine,
With cheeks that make red roses blush,
    a mouth that makes pearls feel shame.
What do you think—will you let this visitor come in?[4]

Though a few of the nineteen known poems by Hafsa are satirical or panegyric, most of her work consisted of love poems. But like Wallada's love story, Hafsa's was a tumultuous one. It was also a sadder tale. Jafar was secretary to the patron of poets and Almohad governor of Granada, Abu Said Uthman. And Uthman was enamored of Hafsa. Governor and secretary competed for Hafsa's attention. Jafar, with poetry as his armor, wrote invective mocking his boss. He is supposed to have asked (with all the racial barbs familiar to us), "What do you see in this dark-skinned man? I can buy you a better man for twenty dinar in the market."

Uthman had Jafar killed. It is hard to feel too sorry for Jafar, but we can certainly feel for Hafsa. Though it was dangerous, Hafsa expressed her grief openly:

They threaten me for mourning a lover they killed by sword.
May God be merciful to one generous with her tears
or to her who cries for one killed by his rivals,
and may the afternoon clouds generously drench the land
wherever she may go.[5]

Hafsa made some unusual choices after her lover's death. She retired from the glittering life of the court she was familiar with, and made a career change from poetry to teaching. In later life, she moved to Marrakesh where she was hired by the caliph, Yaqub al-Mansur, to educate his daughters.

Nazhūn bint al-Garnātiyya al Qulay'iyya (or al-Qalā'i) was also from Granada, but from a less privileged background than Hafsa. More than her poems, Nazhūn the woman seems to have made an impact on the city. She was beautiful and knew reams of poetry by heart. She was also fearless and outspoken, even in public. In fact, she was often called *mājina*—shameless, a buffoon. She exchanged verses with the likes of the wazir Abu Bakr. And in a notorious instance, the beautiful buffoon bared her sharp (and poetic) teeth in an exchange with the blind poet al-Makhzumi in a public gathering at the governor's palace.

Al-Makhzumi recited a poem describing the pleasures of court life as a compliment to his host. Nazhūn was sarcastic. "You compare this court to paradise," she said. "But you, a descendant of the Almodóvar, have grown up among goats and sheep. What do you know about singing and wine and court pleasures?"

The blind poet cleared his throat of phlegm; Nazhūn said, "Stop that."

Al-Makhzumi asked, "Who is this whore?"

"An old woman," answered Nazhūn, "who could have been your mother."

The blind poet snarled, "You lie! This is not the voice of an old woman. I hear the voice of a burning hot whore; I can smell you a mile away."

Several such exchanges followed; then Nazhūn summed it up: "I have repaid a poem with a poem; by my life, tell me now who the best poet is. Although I am a woman by nature, my poetry is masculine."[6]

* * *

Wallada, Muhya, Hafsa, Nazhūn. These Andalusian women were celebrated for more than their poetry in their times. Poets, lovers, trailblazers—they showed medieval Spain what life can be when lived to the fullest; when lived with a certain amount of risk. Their poetry celebrated the rich if tumultuous lives they could choose to lead because of the personal freedoms they enjoyed. Their lives could have only been lived in a tolerant, sophisticated, multicultural society. The status of women has been one important reason scholars have described Andalus as "a place apart" from Medieval Europe and the eastern Muslim lands. A number of women of Islamic Spain—like their counterparts in many premodern Muslim societies—appear to have been active participants in political and cultural affairs. Some, especially those from the affluent class, seem to have enjoyed personal freedoms that would evoke envy in their modern counterparts. This is what helped women like Wallada and Hafsa to shape, in their own small ways, the cosmopolitan civilization associated with Muslims in this particular time and place in history.

And what about the men? What were the dazzling men of this world doing when some of their sisters, mothers, and lovers taught, wrote poetry, and loved?

THE RENAISSANCE MAN CIRCA 12TH CENTURY: DOCTORS WITH MANY NAMES

The Córdoba I saw in 2009 had a full package for tourists—but one ingredient of the package was troublesome for many of the tourists I met. This was philosophy. It is one thing to admire something concrete before you, say a building, however bewildering its history—all that talk of comings and goings, of Visigoths, Muslims, Arabs, Berbers, Christians. But to have to go back to a classroom while on holiday, unravel philosophers, and that, too, of another time...

But it was hard to escape the philosophers who personified the inquiring spirit of the city. They sat stonily in plazas or at the crossroads, gravely considering our antics. Maimonides—or Musa ibn Maimoun—loomed large, especially in the narrow streets of the judería. Then there was Abu 'l-Walid Muhammad ibn Rushd, who came to be known to the West as Averroës.

The first time I met Averroës, I was about fifteen, and in a Manila school that took itself seriously. How do you reconcile logic and Christian theology? This could have been the question that dictated the philosophy class a gaggle of squirming girls was subjected to three times a week. Years later in Córdoba it occurred to me that another question lay hidden: how do you bring together different streams of thought and still ensure that one religion, one part of the world, one tradition, comes out on top?

In Manila, week after week, I was taught scholastic arguments on the existence of God, the existence of the immortal soul, and other such flora and fauna. Thomas Aquinas was the star. Aristotle was an important supporting actor—a flashback to an elderly uncle who had not been redeemed, but had ideas good enough to be called classical. There were also rows of other faces, on marble busts I could just about see in the dimly lit background. Once in a while, I would get to meet these briefly. I met Plato now and then, but never got beyond introductions. Socrates was sent off to the literature class since Aristotle took up all his air. I did meet Averroës; and even our brief meetings made it clear I was expected to remember him, but as an adversary. (Not even the presence of an Indian in class, or the proximity of China and Japan to the Philippines inspired any attention to philosophers from the "east." There was a fifteen-minute Time Out on Oriental Thought, and the Egyptians took up most of that time.)

I would sit in class, writing with supreme confidence in my notebook the scholastic syllogism that proved there is a human soul; then the proof that the soul is immortal. Any other possibility was inevitably reduced, at the end of the argument, to *reductio ad absurdum*. Once the class hour was over, certainty fled in the Manila of the late sixties or in the Indian expat home I lived in. The soul grew pale, joined Socrates and Averroës in the murky shadows in which they lived.

I met Averroës again, all too briefly, in the Bombay of the early seventies—when a stooped old Irish nun called Mother Ward read Chaucer to a group of restless college girls. Mother Ward refused to read the Wife of Bath's tale with us; but the Prologue was permissible, and we discovered, via Chaucer's doctor, that the list of authorities included Averroës:

Well knew he the old Esculapius
And Dioscorides and also Rusus,
Old Hippocras, Hali and Galen
Serapion, Rasis and Avicen,
Averrois, Damascene and Constantine,
Bernard and Gatesden and Gilbertine.

But it was not till 2009 that I finally met the real Averroës—in Córdoba, where he was born and lived as Ibn Rushd.

Abu 'l-Walid Muhammad ibn Rushd (1126–1198) was a doctor and a medical pioneer; a *qadi*, or a chief justice, and a *faqi*, or a jurisprudent; a polymath; a master of philosophy, whether it be logic, Aristotelian philosophy, or Islamic philosophy; a theologian especially interested in dialectics; a student of astronomy, geography, mathematics, physics, and celestial mechanics; a keen follower of psychology, politics, and Arabic music theory. The man even had ideas about cooking, and took the trouble to write about it:

> When [oil] comes from ripe, healthy olives and its properties have not been tampered with artificially, it can be assimilated perfectly by the human body. Food seasoned with olive oil is nutritious, provided the oil is fresh and not rancid. Generally speaking, all olive oil is excellent for people and for that reason in our country it is the only medium needed for cooking meat, given that the best way of preparing it is what we call braising. This is how it is done: Take oil and pour it in a cooking pot. Place the meat

in it and then add hot water, a little at a time, simmering it without letting it boil.[7]

Ibn Rushd wrote more than a hundred books and treatises, and his work survives in Arabic, Latin, and Hebrew. His compendium of medical knowledge was perhaps his most famous work where he lived; he was chiefly known as a medical scholar and practitioner. But his readings of Plato and Aristotle, his commentaries on philosophical questions, would make his work, and his name, travel elsewhere. He would be adopted by places and times other than his own. The medieval European world would turn him into Averroës. There would be enthusiasts, Averroists, who had their own versions of Ibn Rushd's ideas. There would be those who built on his work. But since it had to fit into a Christian framework, he had to be somehow put in the wrong, or at least diminished. Either way, he was valuable. Not only did his work on earlier philosophers and thinkers feed into the hungry mouths of colleges being set up from France to Italy to England, but also his attempt to fit theology, philosophy and science into a Muslim framework would serve as a model for a similar exercise with the Christian framework.

Another court physician, a contemporary of Ibn Rushd's, was also trying to make reason and faith live together in harmony. Born twelve years after Ibn Rushd, Musa ibn Maimoun was referred to as Rabbi Moshe ben Maimon in Hebrew and as Maimonides with a Greek suffix. He wrote, in his mother tongue Arabic, *The Guide for the Perplexed* to resolve any tensions between religious and secular knowledge. Like Ibn Rushd, he adapted Aristotelian thought. And like Ibn Rushd, he wanted science and theology to live together, but in a home made by the teachings of the Torah.

Ibn Rushd and Ibn Maimoun lived in a time when Córdoba's golden period was almost done. The intellectual buzz was still there; religious pluralism and tolerance were still part of the culture of Andalus. But with the Almohad taking over, the question of whether the religious and secular aspects of life could work together had a sharp edge to it. It made sense, for thoughtful men like Ibn Rushd and Ibn Maimoun, to find ways to bring logic and reason into the mix so that differences of faith could be blunted, or temporarily forgotten. They mined all kinds of knowledge to this end; they made copious translations of works from several cultures; they focused on the riches that could be yielded by mathematics, medicine, and astronomy. They collated, combined; but they also created new intellectual possibilities. Both got into trouble for their efforts. Ibn Rushd was exiled from his beloved Andalus when the Caliph was pressured by conservative religious figures to banish him and burn his books on philosophy. Rabbi Musa's books were burned at the order of other rabbis.

Ideas, any breakthrough in knowledge, rarely stand still. And so it was the work of the two Ibns. Their ideas shaped the future of Christianity and the cultural development of Europe. They were the shoots of what would grow into the European Renaissance. But first, their legacies came to a man called Thomas Aquinas, an Italian studying at the University of Paris.

* * *

A worthy triumvirate stands before us: Ibn Rushd the Muslim, Moses Maimonides the Jew, and later, Thomas Aquinas the Christian.

Here is Ibn Rushd, near the Puerta de Almodóvar in Córdoba's old city wall. All images of the man—paintings, statues, are conjectural. The Córdoba statue wears a well-shaped beard, a simple turban, and pointed slippers. The man is alert, ready to get up and make a new point that has just occurred to him. He has, of course, a book with him. It stands on his knee, his left hand holding it in place. Renaissance paintings also pictured Ibn Rushd, though he was far less heroic there. In Andrea di Bonaiuto's "Triumph of St. Thomas Aquinas," a pensive Ibn Rushd bridges "the ancients" of Greece and the European Renaissance—but his place is with the heretics Sabellius and Arius beneath Saint Thomas's throne. In the fresco "The School of Athens," Raphael has a turbaned Ibn Rushd to the lower left, looking over the shoulder of Pythagoras. The center of the painting is taken up by Aristotle and Plato, who walk together.

There, sitting before us in the judería, is Ibn Rushd's comrade, Ibn Maimoun. He, too, is turbaned; he, too, holds a book in his lap. Going by appearances, they could have grown up in the same neighborhood, gone to the same school.

Then there is the youngest of the trio, Thomas Aquinas. He is tall, heavy built; but "straight and well proportioned." His skin has been described as "the color of new wheat." His large head is balding; unlike the other two, he has no turban to hide this sad truth. But all portraits show Aquinas to be noble and meditative, gentle yet strong.

* * *

Our three heroes have quite a bit in common. If they exchanged notes on what exercises their considerable intelligence, they would say in chorus, "the most important relationships of all." State and religion; science and faith; reason and revelation. What knowledge, what salvation is possible, if these couples don't get along? And though they didn't say it in so many words, all three must have known that the acts of probing these relationships, and the understanding that may come of this probing, cannot belong to one city, one language, one people, one faith. This has never been a popular bit of knowledge; our three heroes showed courage in acting on it. Like Ibn Rushd and Ibn Maimoun, who took on the unadventurous conservatives in their time, Aquinas would face the wrath of Church leaders for daring to incorporate the writings of a "pagan"—Ibn Rushd—into Christianity.

Aquinas and the Church made up, of course, and so well that he became a doctor of the Church—*Angelicus Doctor*—and patron of Catholic universities, colleges, and schools throughout the world. Aquinas was hugely indebted to Ibn Rushd and Ibn Maimoun for his intellectual armor. But how was he to purify the power of analysis he was bringing to the centers of learning in the Christian world? He could fend off objections to Aristotle if he constructed a "truer" Aristotle, and reduced Averroës to a useful but imperfect commentator. Aquinas said of Averroës that he was "not so much a Peripatetic as a corruptor of Peripatetic philosophy." It was Aquinas' job to take Aristotle, reason, the whole bag, from "unjust possessors" and deliver it to the home of true revealed religion.

But Ibn Rushd was not talking to Aquinas or his Church. He was talking to and at his own adversaries. There were, of course, the Muslim conservatives of his time, who would anticipate the Church conservatives in accusing Ibn Rushd of mixing up logic and religion, promoting heresy. But Ibn Rushd's warning that a ban on the logical tools of philosophy would be "a wrong to the best sort of people and to the best sort of existing things" was really aimed at someone who lived a century before him. He was talking to *his* powerful bête noire, Abū Hamid al-Ghazālī, who had urged Muslims to take to a mystical path of purification, leaving behind secular learning.

Ghazālī was suspicious of logic, philosophical debate, theological debate, even mathematics. His own debate was with the great earlier Islamic scholars like al-Fārābī and Ibn Sina—Avicenna. Ghazālī practiced what he preached; at the height of a successful academic career, he gave up his professorship in Baghdad and took to the life of an ascetic. In such a life, perhaps, it was possible to believe that a spark on a piece of wood does not cause fire; God does. Indeed, if God wills it, a decapitated man could continue to live. Ibn Rushd's common sense rebelled against this sort of thing. And, he thought, why make it all a conflict between reason and faith? "Truth does not contradict truth."

* * *

Ibn Rushd, chaser of truth, may have been relegated to the background after his time, from the twelfth-century Latin west to my little Catholic school in twentieth-century postcolonial Manila. After Ibn Rushd, that passionate interest in philosophy waned in the world he knew; but found new voices, new vigor, in universities he would have enjoyed in Italy, France, England. His ideas lived on in his avatar as Averroës, though the truth of those ideas shifted ground. Ibn Rushd may not have recognized his voice in these places; or in my Manila or Bombay hundreds of years later. But I suspect he would have pulled out those old tools of logic from the pocket of his robe, gone to work, spoken to me, assumed I would want to speak to him. Ibn Rushd would, perhaps, have forgiven me for not having heard a word in my good school about Andalusian flowering, whether in the sciences or the arts.

I found it hard to give the Andalusia of 2009 the same generous leeway. It seemed to have played the big game of remembering and forgetting so as to keep its everyday face comfortably European. Our old friend and poetic champion, one of the two enamorados, could have been speaking for me, for Wallada, Muhya, Hafsa, Nazhūn, Ibn Rushd and the rest, all of forgotten Spain, all of partially remembered Andalusia, when he wrote of the loss that belongs to all of us:

> *Keeping faith in you,*
> *now you are gone,*
> *is the only creed we could hold,*
> *our religion...*

> *Do not imagine*
> *that distance from you*
> *will change us*
> *as distance changes other lovers.*[8]

7

LOOKING FOR A NATION, LOOKING AT THE NATION

FACE TO FACE WITH MELANCHOLY: ALGIERS 2012

Orhan Pamuk writes of a particular sort of melancholy that he associates with his home, Istanbul. He calls this melancholy *huzun*. I did not pick up on huzun in Istanbul; but I met it face to face, skin to skin, when I saw Algiers—and in celebration. It was July, 2012, and Algeria was celebrating the fiftieth anniversary of its independence from France.

The hotel I was in was a large structure that reminded me of purgatory. It was white, large, and empty. It was also hidden in a cocoon of twisting hilly streets so I could see only blank-faced roofs from my window. The place did not seem convinced it was a hotel; there was none of the usual fuss of either tourism PR or hospitality. If I asked to taste Algerian food, or asked about what to see or do, I got a disinterested, even disappointed look. Everyone seemed preoccupied, in a sad way, as if their energy was concentrated on ways to get out of this halfway house; ways to find their Algeria, which, despite its brave past of fighting for freedom, seemed to have lost its way.

At first I thought it was my ignorance of Arabic; or my rudimentary high school French, confined to the present tense. But when I went out of the hotel—to a conference on the "spirit" of

Frantz Fanon, or simply to look around—I met the same melancholy. It burrowed deep like a soul in the most rousing speech, or the most secretive corners of the casbah, or the prettiest blue-and-white building with grill balconies. This free-floating sadness seemed connected with the state-sponsored security all over the place, and the more informal negotiations of where who could go, where who could swim, what was off-limits outside the city.

Both melancholy and awareness of danger arranged themselves in an incomplete jigsaw puzzle as the days went by. The puzzle made up the picture of a nation continually looking for itself, looking at itself.

This first became apparent in all the talk of Fanon in the seminar room. There were a lot of people there who knew Fanon's work and were deeply interested in what his work had to say for our times. One of Fanon's friends, also one of his biographers, was there; so were his daughter and his son, who took turns attending the seminar. But what I took away from the seminar room was a question. This question looked inward. It was asked in fifty different ways but always with an anxiety that thickened the air. *Have we failed?* Independence, freedom, the Algerian nation: this is what everyone talked about endlessly. But I sensed something held back. There was, for instance, no open talk of relatively recent traumas, the "dirty wars" of the nineties when Algeria was torn apart by the Islamists. I heard little in public about the Islamists.

Then at breakfast one morning, I sat next to Idris, a child psychiatrist. He told me how the fear of being killed had made him move from Algiers to Constantine during the civil war years. He spoke fondly of his eighty-seven-year-old mother—old, he said, not because of her age, but because of what she had lived through. "Her generation lived with enough fear to break anyone's heart, or make them old too soon. As for my friends, many of them died. Those who survived found their lives completely changed." Idris gestured toward one of my new friends, a bubbly woman rushing off to deal with a fresh outbreak of her favorite word, "catastrophe." She had trained to be an archaeologist. But after the turbulent nineties, she had to choose between emigrating if she wanted to be an archaeologist, and staying in Algeria and doing something else.

* * *

In the city, the relics of the past waiting to trip me up were not from the nineties. They were from an older past, and so stale from sitting there that they had grown roots in the landscape.

The car wound its way up hilly roads and hairpin bends to take a small group to the Place des Martyrs. Earlier, by the water, I had seen nameless old houses; broken, dour ruins. "Those were French houses," said Selim, the young Algerian with us. "They broke the foundations before they left so no one else could use the houses." I considered this spiteful departure. Spite is always puzzling in adults; but more puzzling was the fact that these broken houses were still there, moldy leftovers, fifty years later.

All the way uphill was the Notre Dame d'Afrique, visible from most parts of Algiers. The location was spectacular; not just the views, but the quiet, the sense of space, and the yellow mimosas in bloom. The Mediterranean, which was grayish close-up, had turned a luminous blue for the hilltop. Selim showed us how near France is. One of the group muttered that southern Spain seemed closer to him, and it prodded a momentary memory of trade in ideas, refugees, even piracy. But any worthwhile view from Algiers has, clearly, to begin with locating the country that didn't just colonize Algeria but changed the Algerian psyche. We squinted at Marseilles, a straight diagonal line from where we were. It takes just about an hour to fly between the two places; even in 1830, it was easy for pleasure ships to sail from Marseille to watch the drama of the first battle for Algiers. From the safety of the cruise ship, the spectators could, if they wished, look through their opera glasses and see beach-landings, bombardment, slaughtered corpses along the coastline.

Inside the Notre Dame d'Afrique, models of ships hung in three corners, as if to remind the pieds noirs, the shoe-clad French settlers in Algeria, that heaven is elsewhere. Or that home means travel. Or that home is in two places: France was close enough, but meanwhile, France in Algeria was home. The call to *Priez pour nous et por les musulmans* was inscribed above the main altar; and to the left was a more general invocation to fraternal amity, in both French and Arabic. But our guide Selim was not thinking of the French. Or the French and Algerian periods had collapsed in time in his head. In the nineties, he told us, there were police here, in this church, to protect the priests.

On our way out, the esplanade drew us again. We looked at the mothers watching their children at play; they were there for the terrace, not the church. We turned back to the view.

In the 1840s, European travelers nearing Algiers were tantalized by what they saw. From the deck of their steamers, they saw the "Pirate's Daughter," one of the nicknames they gave Algiers. The city hung before them, "a triangular shape of chalk on a slope of green hills, the dark Atlas mountains rising menacingly in the distance behind."[1]

But it was 2012, and Selim was gesturing downhill. "This used to be a ninety percent Jewish area," he said. He pointed out the Jewish cemetery, a synagogue nearby, and a Christian graveyard at some distance. "The synagogue is empty," Selim told us. The Jews, he said, used to speak dialects of Arabic, but then switched to French even before they emigrated. "They left in the sixties. And those who are still here," he added, his face carefully neutral, "are hiding."

The next day, I saw the best places to hide in Algiers. I climbed the steps of the Casbah that begins high in the hills and rambles downward to the sea. This old Ottoman city, which fascinated and frightened the French, is now a warren of narrow streets with mostly shabby houses, some covered with tin sheets. There was an air of neglect; I thought I could smell something bleak, but I wasn't sure if it was the sewage, or the burden of too many pasts. I went up a stretch with old men sitting on wooden benches on either side, smoking, drinking tea. They seemed to have sat there forever, literally watching life pass by so they could give it a bad review. A gaggle of children ran down the steps at breakneck speed, shouting *Salaam alaikum!* as they rushed past me. My heart rose; the old men and I looked at them till they were out of sight. Far from the children and old men, high on the hill, I noticed a fort-like structure with cannons. It loomed large and forbidding; it was there, I was told, so the French could keep an eye on the Casbah. Down the slope, all the way to the sea, white buildings had been built to screen the Casbah. Algiers then got a new nickname: la Blanche, the white one.

* * *

At dinner that night, in a grand official building that must have been a close relative of my hotel, a friendly professor of sociology translated the speeches in Arabic. (In between, he amused me by translating the mock-lyrical effusions of an Egyptian writer who was declaring his passion for every woman in sight.) But when someone admired the professor's Arabic, he said, "I am Berber." And to emphasize what that meant in the official melting pot of the Algerian nation, he added, rather sharply, "We have our own language. Tamazight. The Berber languages at one time covered the entire Maghreb and the Sahara, but Arabic came in from the Middle Ages. Even now, with all the state-sponsored Arabization, we make up one-fourth of the population."

I found out that at least six Berber languages are spoken in Algeria. Of these various groups, the largest in number, the Berbers in Kabylia, have also been the most vocal about their survival. After protests in 2002, Berber acquired legal status as an "official language." But this has not necessarily meant acceptance. Berber languages are not taught in schools; official documents are generally accepted only in Arabic. In fact, in 2008 and 2009, the police came down hard on attempts to organize Berber language congresses.

I was learning this huge nation in small fragments; but one thing was clear. Conflict—or to be precise, war—has multiple meanings in Algeria. And it lives simultaneously in multiple points of time.

To begin with, Algeria was a favored site for testing out a "science of war" specially constructed for Africa. In 1847, the influential French political thinker Alexis de Tocqueville (1805–1859) wrote,

> Experience has not only shown us where the natural theater of war is located. It has also taught us to make war. It has revealed the strengths and weaknesses of our adversaries. It has made us understand how to beat them and, once beaten, how we should keep the upper hand. It can now be said that war in Africa is a science. Everyone is familiar with its rules and everyone can apply those rules with almost complete certainty of success. One of the greatest services that Field Marshal Bugeaud has rendered his country is to have spread, perfected and made everyone aware of this new science.[2]

The French military—Bugeaud and company—applied the new science on the ground. As governor-general of Algeria, Bugeaud tested his system of flying columns, the *razzia* tactic, and made it standard operation. During one particular razzia, the Arab tribes fled with their women and children and hid in caves. The French officers ordered the Arabs to surrender; the natives refused. The officers ordered their men to light fires, then seal the exits.

The French conquerors tortured, massacred, smoked out, and deported villagers; they scorched the earth as policy and burned harvests; they seized land; they emptied granaries. By the time the people were thoroughly subjected, they had been reduced to half their numbers by war, famine, and disease. The social and economic basis of Algerian life was destroyed.

Once conquest was achieved, colonization was next. Restricted at first, then total. The colons, the settlers, came in and made *their* Algeria. Two separate systems of life were set up, distinguished by race, culture and religion.

These are the historical facts. But behind these facts, on the real-life stage, there were people acting and being acted upon. Bugeaud wielded the sword or the gun or the fire—or the men wielding the weapons. But there were other actors, men like de Tocqueville, who fought a more invisible war of ideas and policy and politics. I found them more puzzling. A man who believed in liberty and equality, who wrote about it day after day: How did he live with his desire for a colony, for *subjects*?

LOOKING FOR LIBERTY AND EQUALITY: WARRIORS IN THEORY, WARRIORS IN PRACTICE

It is 1840. The second volume of *Democracy in America*, his opus for posterity, has just been published. Alexis-Charles-Henri de

Tocqueville, son of aristocratic parents who narrowly escaped the guillotine, has become the prophet of equality. The two volumes sit on his desk to one side, solid evidence of his love for liberty. He has written on how a country, a people, should live.

He has written eloquently of his own high standards for a civilized nation. Human equality is "universal and permanent." He has questioned Arthur de Gobineau, who wrote on the inequality of the human races: "Can you not see that your doctrine naturally gives rise to all the evils bred by permanent inequality: arrogance, violence, contempt toward others who are like oneself, tyranny, and wretchedness of all kinds"?[3] As for liberty, de Tocqueville has written, "the greatest and most irreparable calamity for a people is to be conquered."[4]

But even before he completed *Democracy in America*, de Tocqueville had a very different place on his mind: Algeria, taken in 1830, and under "limited" occupation for a decade now. He had written long newspaper articles; his name had become known to voters, which is what he intended. Since his election to the Chamber of Deputies in 1839, he has become an expert on Algerian matters. He can see, more than the other deputies, how important Algeria is to France.

Should that insight, that ethical awareness he felt in America, be applied to North Africa? Force and exploitation do things to the subjects, but also to those who are subjecting them. What they do is barbaric; it cannot be a part of civilization, a thing de Tocqueville is in love with but can also analyze. When he looks closely at the Indian sepoys rising against the British, he is able to see that "foreign settlers injure, or seem to injure in a thousand ways the private interests that are precious to all mankind... I don't doubt that in Algeria the Arabs and the Kabyles are more irritated by the presence of our settlers than by our soldiers."[5]

The Indian situation floats again into his mind. Despite this incident of the sepoys, there's no doubt that the British have done it. A small island has drawn all eyes on itself, shown the world how a European power can dominate a huge number of non-Christian natives far away. The France he knew at one time, the France he hopes to help make, will be overtaken. He feels a wave wash over him; it makes him feel far too many things at once, anxiety, longing, ambition. He bends his head, gives in to it: "Those notions of liberty and equality which everywhere are shaking or destroying slavery—who propagated them throughout the world?... It cannot be denied that we ourselves did so. This has been the source both of our glory and our force."[6] And, "with time, perseverance, skill and justice, there is no reason we cannot raise on the coast of Africa a great monument to the glory of our country."[7]

He, too, must have a particle of this glory, the author of *Democracy*, build on it for a new grandeur. He's a Frenchman, a French politician. A choice has to be made. Action needs to be taken. Besides, "due to the simple fact of the superiority of its knowledge, a people as powerful and civilized as our own will exercise an almost invincible influence over peoples that are small and nearly barbarian; for these peoples to become incorporated into our own, we need only establish durable relations with them."[8]

* * *

In 1841, Tocqueville finally saw the "experiment"—the colony that had taken up so much space in his head. His preparation was not enough to protect him from feeling astonished; disoriented. He let go his idea of turning Algerians into Frenchmen: that was "a fantasy that only a person who has not been there could dream up."[9] He took careful notes, met settlers, civil servants, a bishop, and, of course, military men. He went on a field trip with Bugeaud. His admiration for Bugeaud came and went, but he thought the military officers crude and violent, unfit to govern. Still, when he returned to France in a month—his visit cut short by illness—he wrote:

> In France I have often heard people I respect, but do not approve, deplore [the army] burning harvests, emptying granaries and seizing unarmed men, women and children. As I see it, these are unfortunate necessities that any people wishing to make war on the Arabs must accept... I believe the laws of war entitle us to ravage the country and that we must do this, either by destroying crops at harvest time, or all the time by making rapid incursions, known as raids, the aim of which is to carry off men and flocks.[10]

Later, in 1847, he would warn his countrymen that if their methods in Algeria did not change, the last chapter of colonization would be soaked in blood. Despite this grim warning (which went unheard), and despite the fact that the last act was indeed bloody, it is not de Tocqueville's prophetic abilities that are striking. It's the fact that even for the democrat Tocqueville, the map of the world was white in color and firmly affixed to Europe. Those signposts of civilization, liberty and equality, were applicable to people. And it was in Europe, finally, that you had people; the rest of the world had natives.

* * *

White people, black natives; colonizer, colonized. History has made these charged words commonplace. But so many of us live out the aftermath of what these words did to us. We may bandage it with the word *post*colonial, or push it all back into the remote past. Still the colonized soul is not easily shed. Frantz Fanon, champion of liberation, warned of this, but he was talking of his time, a time of the "simple" colonial subject.

That dominated colonial subject had two ways of survival. (The third, a willing party to oppression, was clearly not an option.) One was to live in the colonizer's world, make the colonizer-country his own. This was not impossible. In the case of Algeria, for example, there was the French colonial doctrine of "La France d'Outre-mer": "The colony was to become an integral, if non-contiguous, part of the mother country, with its society and population made over... in her image."[11] The result was a confusion every colonized person is intimate with:

> The trouble is, they have been told they were French. They learned it in school. In the barracks. (Where they were given shoes to wear on their feet.) On the battlefields. They have had France squeezed into them wherever, in their bodies and in their souls...[12]

So the colonized could speak French, know French history and literature, go to France, live and work there, fall in love, have children. But there was a difficulty: something would remain between him and the really French. This is what Frantz Fanon, who went from Martinique to France and fought for the Free French forces, lived in the step-mother country as a student then a psychiatrist, found. There were the colonizers and the colonized, and a cold gray sea spread between them. This sea could sometimes be navigated, but it was choppy all the same.

So, the second way to survive as a colonized subject: Fanon shaped the anger he came to know intimately into a theory of liberation. A way for the wretched of the earth to survive oppression and grow fully human again. Fanon wanted to act against colonialism, but he also wanted to unravel the *psychology* of colonialism.

* * *

Algeria, 1954. A slim, dark, elegantly dressed man sits at his desk. Frantz Fanon is not happy sitting still; and he hates being alone. He would rather walk about the room, dictating, his arms in constant movement, his hand grabbing bits of air as if they are words or metaphors. But tonight he is alone and he has something to say. The thoughts are bubbling to the surface.

The words sputter out of his pen in staccato bursts. Accounts of the tortured men he listens to in the Blida-Joinville hospital; what he has learned about skin, the color of skin. What it does to people, black or white. What the dominated man or woman can do to put himself or herself together again. He writes:

I want my voice to be harsh, I don't want it to be beautiful, I don't want it to be pure, I don't want it to have all dimensions.

I want it to be torn through and through, I don't want it to be enticing, for I am speaking of man and his refusal, of the day-to-day rottenness of man, of his dreadful failure.

I want you to tell.

That I should say for example: ...[13]

He pauses to rein in the images, sort out the army riding into his head.

Millions of fellahs exploited, cheated, robbed.
Fellahs grabbed at four in the morning,
Released at eight in the evening.
From sun to moon.
Fellahs gorged with water, gorged with leaves, gorged with
old biscuit which has to last all month.
Motionless fellah and your arms move and your bowed back
but your life stopped. The cars pass and you don't move. They
could run over your belly and you wouldn't move.
Arabs on the roads.
Sticks slipped through the handle of the basket.
Empty basket, empty hope, this whole death of the fellah.
Two hundred fifty francs a day.
Fellah without land.
Fellah without reason.[14]

It's been only a year since Fanon met Algeria face to face, but it takes up all his time. He does not know Arabic or Berber; but he knows, he can *feel* the anger and passion and longing of his friends in the Front de Libération Nationale. More and more they are becoming his own. In his short time in Algeria he has seen how battle against the French has torn tradition apart. He has seen how men and women, their families and children, now connect with each other as they share battle. He thinks of it as a "radical mutation," this ripple effect of the hunger for freedom. And he wants to do more than celebrate this radical mutation; he wants to find ways to let this mutation go deeper. National liberation, yes. It must be fought for; it must be won. But it is no victory if it does not change the place, if it does not reach other places. The call to freedom must rest on that bedrock of all action, an ideology. What kind of organization will demand a freedom that must come with sweeping change?

The raging war of independence has become the center point of his life. He does not know how long he will be able to keep his job in the hospital. He wants to change things at the hospital, where both Algerian and French patients hold up a depressing mirror to everything wrong with the colony. But he can't keep at it if he is to do more for the freedom fighters. He can't, for example, continue to treat the French soldiers and officers broken by their job, which is to break Algerians. (But Fanon, who will later be considered by some to be the apostle of violence, treats both sets of patients with equal concern.)

It's late at night, but he has not yet thought of bed. His days are full; and tonight, like most nights, the day is not yet done. Luckily he can make do with just a couple of hours of sleep. There's too much to do, writing, talking, asking questions; squeezing every drop of life out of every moment in the present.

There's a past, too. He is still young, very young, but he has enough of a past; many pasts. To himself at least, he can talk about the past that has marked him forever.

Martinique. How far away that childhood in an island "department" seems. His mother's shop, his father's customs job, his own lycée where he read hungrily and played football. Almost comfortable, his place in the island. But all human relations were tightly pigeonholed into boxes labeled with shades of pigmentation, the darker-skinned weighing down to the bottom, the lighter-skinned floating to the top. In this brutally drawn map of difference, he had been taught to believe he was almost French, and he had almost believed it; then he met his poet-teacher, Aimé Césaire. "No race," said Césaire, "has a monopoly of beauty, or intelligence, or strength, and there will be a place for all at the rendezvous of victory."

Fanon conjures up that eighteen-year-old self of his, questioning, confused, leaving Martinique in the waning days of the war to fight with the Free French forces. On the one hand, all those brave ideas he had learned in school, ideas of equality and fraternity born of the French Revolution and the enlightenment; on the other hand, the reality that betrayed these ideas. Even now, that betrayal feels like acid on his tongue. He can still see those scenes as they invaded from the south of France: fighting in snow, which he had never seen before; the Senegalese troops pulled back because they could not be allowed to liberate France; being reclassified as white somehow. Black, then not black. French, then not French. He remembers the letter he wrote his parents: "If one day you should hear that I died facing the enemy, never say: he died for the good cause."

The confusion he felt then, and later when he worked in France, gave birth to a new Frantz, not disconnected from the old one. This new Frantz did not rush home. Home, Martinique, was too small now for his questions.

He sees himself again, the student of medicine in Lyon, mining everything he has seen and read and heard, mining words, poetry, rhythm, to look at the "lived experience of a black person." And he had seen, with piercing clarity, that if the black man was imprisoned in his blackness by the racist eye, the white man was trapped in his whiteness. Only that glimmer of humanity, when recognized, could set both free.

No Negro mission then, no white burden, only freedom. That's when he first began to grapple seriously with freedom, the key to it. He couldn't see kindness or charity or benevolence opening the black prison; in fact, no one could open that prison but the prisoner. The prisoner had to seize the key with a violence that would restore his humanity to him.

The testimony of the past brings Fanon back to the demands of the Algerian night in the present. Violence: what he is now thinking about it, saying, writing, will later arm all kinds of people, their movements. But now, sitting alone in the night, it is Fanon the pragmatist who is considering the violence necessary to overthrow colonizers who are anything but non-violent. And he is not thinking of violence by itself but as a part of struggle. Struggle is the collective key. As for him, the key is shaped like a question mark. That final line of his first book echoes inside him like a lantern that will guide him through the darkest night. "My final prayer: oh my body, make me always a man who asks questions."

* * *

Fanon packed as much as possible into what was to be a short life; he was driven by the need to *do* something. He wanted to take up arms in 1955, but the FLN assured him they had enough volunteers. Instead, he celebrated the ways in which ordinary Algerians took part in the revolution. Fanon the doctor insisted that the struggling people were being transformed and "re-celebralized" even in their private lives as men and women. Taking part in the war amounted to acts of liberation, especially for Algerian women.

Acts of liberation. To begin with, there was liberation and liberation. The French government, as part of their "pacification" campaign, appealed to "French Muslim" women to emancipate themselves. The means offered: literacy classes, the vote, the French marriage law, even an event to unveil in public. (Apparently some of the women coaxed or bullied into this event had never worn a veil in the first place.) The campaign had little success, but it was ambitious enough for the FLN to respond. They said that women would be liberated when Algeria was liberated; but they also rediscovered women's commitment to the cause.

Whatever the theory-policy-rhetoric, whoever the narrative was coming from, the women warriors were there. There were individual heroines, but on the whole, both theory and practice of battle was somewhat different when it came to women. Women in the mountains and the rural areas and the city cared for the fighters, male or female. We know some of their names, sometimes only the first name or the last name. Both the named and unnamed made up the invisible essential base of the war.

"Sometimes we cooked all night for the *Moudjahidines*, the women fighters. At night they slept, and we kept watch over them. They slept in blockhouses [underground hiding places] outside the village: it was we who used to camouflage the blockhouses, covering them with earth and bramble. We would then leave, carrying a bag full of branches to cover our tracks. At dawn we used to look hard to see that the mountain was not inhabited by soldiers, if they had not lit fires."[15]

The women did the everyday things needed to make a revolution: they cooked; they nursed; they were dressmakers. "We were constantly changing men's clothes, dyeing their hair and ours, too, and doing our best to reduce the risk of being found out by the enemy. All this was thought of and carried out by women."[16]

Once the FLN decided to involve women more directly in their urban operations, they became couriers of messages and arms; they were lookouts; they hid militants or traveled with them. A few planted bombs.

The veil and *haïk* became weapons of war. If they were shed, it was not for the reason given by the French women's liberation campaign, but to pass more easily through barricades to the French quarter. If they had to appear "western," they took off the veil. "I had to go unnoticed, be taken for a French person, so as not to arouse any suspicions, since anybody who looked like an Arab was searched and arrested. So, I used to put on make-up and dress in the French way."[17]

Some of the women wore the veil they were used to, except this veil had turned militant. But there were others, who had been to French schools and were not used to the veil, who now wore it if it helped carry money, messages, or bombs from one part of Algiers to another. "Our brothers wouldn't have been able to carry out their work without us... because we could go out wearing the veil."[18] Indeed, wearing veils helped men on occasion. "Our lives were like theirs, but our activities could be more adventurous because we could go out wearing the veil. They were the ones shut up at home. Once, we dressed them up in veils to go outside; they had to dress up like us if they wanted to go out."[19]

The women took supplies to prisoners, often their sons or husbands; they attended their trials. They made a link between the resistance and the places of incarceration. In Algiers, this was more often than not the Barberousse, the prison on the outskirts of the Casbah. "When curfew was lifted, we wives and mothers would visit our loved ones. If we saw water flowing under the enormous gate, we knew some of our people had been executed. The water must have been used to wash away their blood. We would race to the gate, to the white sheet of paper pinned there with a list of names. Some of us would be afraid of whose names we would find. Once we read the names, fear left us. We would stay close to the martyrs' relatives and walk them home. We would let everyone know who had been executed, how many of our people had been martyred."[20] And though women had not attended burials, the war changed that, too; they joined the demonstrations held at the burial of dead fighters.

When there was a call to strike, like the seven-day strike, the women went from terrace to terrace, urging people to join the strike: "For the first two days, it went perfectly in the casbah: everything was closed and nobody left their homes. But the paras [French paratroopers] broke into people's houses and smashed shop windows and, on the third day, people began to come out. We suggested to Saadi [FLN commander Youssef Saadi] that we should go from terrace to terrace to talk to women...After about half an hour, the paras arrived. When they tried to come after us, women helped us to escape by taking us from one terrace to another."[21]

Escape was not always possible; some of the women were caught. The arrested women were taken to one of the dark (though not so secret) places, like the Barberousse. In the Barberousse prison, the women's block was right next to the entrance. When the guillotine came at daybreak, the women would be the first to hear the heavy prison gate being opened, the grating noise it always made. There was only one way they could support the men who were to be executed: they would burst into song. It was almost uplifting, these moments of solidarity. The rest, suffered alone, was far from uplifting, for both torturer and tortured.

Fanon was categorical on what this torture was all about. "Torture in Algeria is not an accident, or an error, or a fault. Colonialism cannot be understood without the possibility of torturing, of violating, or of massacring. Torture is an expression and a means of the occupant-occupied relationship.[22] And after 1954, torture rose to "the level of a system."[23] The system: being forced to strip, beatings. Water treatment, electric shock. Rape, sometimes rape with objects like a broken bottle. "When I endured the pain from my torturers' blows, I was sure that we no longer belonged to the human species."[24]

* * *

The passion for freedom is a heady thing, though, and even prison, even torture, cannot always stifle it. And liberty and equality are often too big for the small maps drawn by nationality. A diary entry kept by a woman prisoner in the Barberrouse reveals how she combined her French education and her nationalist upbringing: "Even when I was very young I already knew the principles established by the French Republic of 1789, Liberty, Equality and Fraternity, which have dominated the political and social landscape. Moreover, the history lessons that I received at school clearly showed me that nationalist and revolutionary movements were in no way considered subversive. On the contrary, all my textbooks spoke of those who wished to shake off the yoke of foreign domination with admiration and respect."[25]

Twenty years later, the same woman, Baya, was still fighting, but it was a somewhat different fight. In the film "The Battle of Algiers," an ideologue of the freedom movement tells Ali le Pointe in words reminiscent of Fanon: It is hard to begin a revolution. It's harder to sustain it. It's only afterward, once the revolution is won, that the real difficulties begin...

Twenty years later, Baya Hocine was in the Algerian National Assembly debating the introduction of a Family Code.[26] She argued against the Code, saying that this would reduce women to the status of minors for life. She was booed and shouted down by male deputies. By the time the Family Code was passed in 1984, Baya Hocine was no longer part of either the National Assembly or the FLN. She died abroad in 2000. When her body came home to Algeria, it was received by a small group of women—her "former cellmates and sisters-in-arms."

The memory of what they fought for was, perhaps, not yet a memory, because they still had to fight for it. What they fought for: "being ourselves, not having to judge ourselves by a reference."[27] The fight would continue fifty years later.

FREEDOM TURNS FIFTY

July 5, 2012. Like the other participants at the Fanon conference in Algiers, I, too, had an official-looking invitation for the evening's celebration of fifty years of freedom. For several days, the newspapers had been talking of the "major festivals" being organized by the authorities; workers were reportedly working nonstop to raise banners of celebration.

But despite the hoisted flags along the waterfront, I did not sense any spontaneous festive spirit. In the Casbah, old men sat around drinking tea as usual. Children raced down the interminable steps as if they couldn't wait to get to their future. No one in the narrow old heart of Algiers seemed to think the birthday party had anything to do with them.

I heard that in circles more privileged than the Casbah, the planned celebrations had been criticized for being "populist." Like the Algerian speakers in the Fanon conference, the non-government political class wanted to debate freedom—what had been achieved in fifty years, where they had gone wrong. Some intellectuals had spoken of "revolutionary legitimacy." Though politicians claimed this legitimacy had passed— President Bouteflika famously said, "Our time is over"—the major political and security posts continued to be held by those who took part in the freedom movement. For now, no one was paying much attention to the intellectuals; the officials were preoccupied with the controversy over payments to performers in the celebrations.

* * *

Getting into the open-air stadium left me with a sense of achievement, so frighteningly thorough was the security we had to get past to get into the place. There was already a huge crowd, and there was the confusion of finding places on the packed bleachers so we could sit together as a group. The Indians in the group, used to large numbers, were blasé about the turnout; still it was impressive. Everywhere I turned I saw young faces. I had noticed that the city was full of young men, walking arm in arm, or just sitting around, smoking. But concentrated in this enclosed space, the number of youths was dramatic confirmation of the fact that this is a truly young nation.

Soon the French were onstage. French Algeria unfolded through the actors in the foreground, evocative old photos and film footage behind them like a supporting cast. Throughout, there were steps in the background; the Casbah was always there. I thought of the hole-in-the-wall café I had visited in the Casbah: the walls inside were lined with solemn black-and-white photographs of heartbreakingly young men and women. The café owner pointed out a woman who had thrown grenades. Her eyes were unsmiling and innocent, fixed on a spot we could not see. Martyred as they were, she and her comrades were going to remain young and hopeful.

I looked at the actors strutting about the stage now, giving orders, keeping *their* Algeria in order. It was only in 1999 that the French government admitted to a war. Till then the reasoning was that France could not have gone to war with a part of its own territory. And if there was a war, it had to remain nameless. Better still, it had to be masked, as incidents, events, terrorist action. Even after the 1999 admission, Algeria—the colonization, the war—remains a past which does not pass. *Un passé qui ne passe pas.* In 2005, the French parliament passed a law that textbooks should show the "positive role" France had played in its former colonies; the law was later rescinded. To mark this fiftieth year, an exhibition in the French Army Museum in Paris was showing a video of the torture of a French soldier by FLN fighters. In a corner of the same exhibition hung three grainy photos of French soldiers torturing an Algerian. (The photographer, Jean-Philippe Charbon, had refused to allow these photos to be published in his lifetime.)

Both sides have great difficulty managing memory. "We see that the more time passes, the more memory returns," said French historian Benjamin Stora.

Sitting in the stadium, it was possible to feel a different poignancy. This could be one of the last times the aging revolutionaries in the audience relived what they had done, and what was done to those they knew among the one and a half million who died between 1954 and 1962.

The air was thickening with nostalgia. The crowds cheered as victory was within arm's reach onstage. Then, on a crescendo, the word *freedom* appeared on the stage and the screens. The crowds erupted. The young men who had not seen French Algeria were on their feet, dancing without inhibition. They waved cell phones so the stadium turned psychedelic with light. Some shouted patriotic slogans. The girls clapped and cheered them on.

Freedom had been won. Now the spectacle onstage had to turn to the less stirring business of nation-building. I didn't need to know Arabic to understand the official-speak that followed. Throughout my childhood, seeing a film in an Indian movie theater meant sitting through the dull but worthy black and white nation-building reel first. Hospitals, dams, ribbons being cut by our beloved leaders, that sort of thing; everything that told you were being looked after by the big state which is your guardian, your mother and father. We may no longer take this as a given, but remembering that faith leaves you feeling wistful. But, I told myself, this remembering is different in

India and Algeria. Not only did they have very different colonial experiences, they also went down somewhat different paths as they made up their new, free nations.

Where were they to begin in 1962, as the Algerian nation waited to be constructed? "Colonization brought the genocide of our identity, of our history, of our language, of our traditions," President Bouteflika once said.[28] It must have been daunting, facing the ruins of a land devastated by colonization, trying to make up a ready-made identity. In 1964, Algerian psychiatrist Khaled Benmiloud wrote that "Algerians knew what they no longer were, but did not have a clear idea of who they were."[29]

One thing was clear: the new Algeria had to be antithetical to what France was perceived to be. The official Algerian identity took to heart the cultural anticolonialism of Abdelhamid Ben Badis, founder of the 1930s religious reformist movement, the *ulama*: "Arabic is my language; Algeria is my country; Islam is my religion." In 1963, Islam was declared the state religion and Arabic the national language; and a program of Arabicizing all national institutions was begun.

The irony was that there was something of the French nation about all this, drowning all tongues in the official sea of one language, for example.

As long as the French were the enemy, the battleground was relatively uncrowded; the mess of many sides did not have to be dealt with. The war veterans, through the FLN, were to be the only representatives of the people in a single-party state. It continued as a dominant force in the eighties despite more space for pluralism. But by then it had become what disenchanted

Algerians call *le pouvoir*, "a politico-military regime incorporating a complex web of army generals, politicians and businessmen, monopolizing power and exchanging privileges, favors and shady deals in order to keep a stranglehold on power."[30]

The nation was no longer new. That old revolutionary activism had frayed, ossified in office. New activisms slipped into the empty spaces onstage. In an ironic recycling of revolutionary writing, the fundamentalist Islamique de Salut (FLS) used Fanon's writings on violence to justify their attacks on the Algerian regime.

Onstage, too, we had moved on to the nineties, the decade of the dirty war. The same reticence I had sensed earlier in the week came back. The tableaux on stage became stylized, with black hoods and shadows flitting from table to table in a city café, as if terrorism is that which must not be named.

The Algerian sitting next to me gave up on translating and interpolated his own text. And he fast-forwarded to the less dirty but still unfulfilled present.

"We have the oil and gas, we are rich," he whispered to me. "But these young people"—and he waved at the boys around us, no longer dancing, "what do we tell them about the Islamists, or the corruption, or the leaders who only want us to remember them as revolutionaries?"

Onstage the evening went on with songs and speeches, flags and dancers. But the fervor was gone out of it. The revolution remained unfulfilled.

* * *

It was strange going back to hearing about Fanon the next day in the seminar room. I couldn't help noticing that Fanon was absent the evening before. There was not even one measly little quote.

In an interview, Fanon biographer David Macey said:

> I'm not sure that Fanon is sufficiently 'present' in Algerian memories to be an embarrassment. He is, of course, 'commemorated' from time to time. In any case, commemoration is not necessarily the same thing as 'remembering'... If Fanon were remembered in Algeria, he probably would be an embarrassment in that his vision of the post-independent period departs significantly from that of the FLN... Fanon is a distant reminder that there could have been a different Algeria.[31]

On my last day in Algiers, I was told a story about Fanon's widow. After his death, Fanon's French wife Josie stayed on in Algeria. In 1988, the story goes, she watched from the balcony of her flat as the army shot down demonstrating workers and youth in the street below. She is supposed to have sighed, "Ah Frantz, the wretched of the earth again." Her despair at where freedom had gone was apparently one reason for her suicide soon after.

Stories aside, the revolutionary past aside, I sensed, in Algiers in 2012, a unique version of the waiting that goes on in so many postcolonial countries: waiting for the nation they were supposed to have got.

8

BITTERSWEET DANISH

COPENHAGEN 2012:
ORGANIC AND BOTANICAL LIVING

It was a crisp cool Sunday morning in Copenhagen. The girl at the hotel desk, half Thai, half Indian, told me she is Danish because she "thinks like a European." She also told me the botanical gardens were not far from the hotel. For some reason, possibly postcolonial, I have always felt compelled to visit all botanical gardens. I set out to add this one to my list. On the way, I passed several locked churches. In St. Andreas Kirke, the lone open cathedral I found, a volunteer worker told me that seven more city churches would soon close down. "Where's the money?" she asked with a wry shrug. Between the cathedral and the gardens, I got some idea of where the money might be. I passed an extraordinary number of spas, physiotherapy clinics, massage parlors, all sorts of places with all sorts of bodily therapies on offer. A beauty salon advertised organic hairdressing. The neighborhood store, manned by an Afghan and an Iraqi, sold organic vegetables, fruits, teas, dates. The roads and the pavements bordering the canals were filled with stern skinny people running with religious fervor.

The botanical gardens, too, had people running for organic

purposes. I sat down on a bench, tired from the sight of so much exertion. I watched a glossy magpie pecking at a well-packed plastic bag full of garbage, probably organic. The Danish call the magpie skade. Skade, it turns out, has two meanings in Danish—"damage" as well as "top" or "treetop." When I got up, the skade hopped a few feet away and gave me an evil look. I recalled the Irish nursery rhyme about the magpie:

> *One is for sorrow, two is for joy*
> *Three is a girl, four is a boy*
> *Five is for silver, six is for gold*
> *Seven is a story, never to be told.*

My skade decided I was harmless and hopped back to the garbage bag. This city bird will eat almost anything, hence its bad reputation. But the skade is too ordinary to be the star of the botanical gardens.

In June 2012, a plant native to the rainforests of Sumatra flowered in Copenhagen. The plant is called *Amorphophallus Titanum*—in Danish, this means the greatest mutable penis; in Latin, giant shapeless penis. It smells like a carcass, so it is also called the corpse-flower. Reminiscent of nineteenth-century adverts for new wonders in the Tivoli, newspapers and the net wrote, blogged, photographed and video-lapsed breathlessly: A most amazing flower has blossomed! The queue at the gardens was longer than a hundred and fifty meters as people stood in line to see and smell the organic wonder. One gardener slept in the gardens, afraid to miss the actual flowering.

Flowers, stories—strange things from other places have always found a responsive audience here. It is a way to go elsewhere without leaving home.

GOING ELSEWHERE, CIRCA NINETEENTH CENTURY

I was at a bookshop that supplemented mere books with ethnic beads and bangles, scarves, exotic objects from Africa and Asia. A woman I met explained it to me: "Denmark is dull and boring. We need to go somewhere else, or bring other places here." She looked apologetic but also matter-of-fact: It's obvious, she seemed to say. We need elsewhere to complete us.

The woman's ancestors knew this more than a century back. The fascination for elsewhere began in the eighteenth century, but it was in the nineteenth century that parks, bazaars, novels, operas, popular music, interior decoration, science, travelogues, exhibitions, funfairs, buildings, department stores, paintings, and magazines together made up a full-blown Danish experience of the Orient. This Orient was often frankly fantastic; sometimes pretend-realistic; but it was always new, strange, sumptuous.

Victor Hugo summed it up for Europe in his 1829 prologue to the collection of poems, *Les Orientales*: "We are all Orientalists now." The "all" included scientists, explorers, businessmen, artists, poets, colonialists. Hugo's oriental poems were written when France had already begun its project of settler colonialism in Algeria. But the Orient that flourished in nineteenth-century Denmark was not always easily mapped. In his 1889 *Poems from the Levant*, Holger Drachmann explained that the Orient of poets could not be located like the Orient of geographers. Unlike the geographical Orient, the poetic orient is not to be found "on those meridians, with those people in those cities, with those narrow streets"; but in a place in "which you find [the Orient] in the song of the poet rather than... the map of the country."[1] The idea was to bring Aladdin to Denmark, rub his magic lamp, and summon a truly enjoyable Orient at home. Aladdin, Alā-ad-Dīn or Alauddin in Arabic, means "nobility of faith," but the new version of the name could live in less exalted territory.

I got a quick taste of the enjoyable Orient in 2012 when I found a cozy bar one evening on Vendersgade. The bar offered several vaguely "eastern" dishes, the sort that can be described as anything from vegetarian to "Hare Krishna" but has little to do with anything eaten in the East. The food came in western-size portions and was wholesome. And the place was comfortable. The wooden benches and chairs were piled with satiny cushions. Their backs were draped with shawls and scarves that the bar clientele could use to be snug, or to imagine themselves in an oriental Neverland. It made me believe an Aladdin or two may show up to have a drink with me if I waited long enough.

BETWEEN WORLDS, 1844, 2012: MERMAIDS AND MERMAID-MAKERS IN CONVERSATION

It is 1844, and two Danish Aladdins walk into a Copenhagen café. It is the time of day when the café is full. Conversations are in full flow as glasses are filled with wine; there is a hint of romance between the young man and woman who sit close together. A sad old man sits alone puffing at his pipe, his face fixed in disapproval. Whatever they are doing, everyone is aware of the two men who have just entered the café and insisted on getting the best table by the window. The young men in the café, looking for models, stare at the newcomers openly. Others are more discreet. The two men whom everyone is looking at wear red fez caps; one of them is an outright dandy. It is hard to make out whether his clothes (and his manner) come from Paris or from someplace with a long sibilant Eastern name.

It is a pleasant day in late summer, just the right evening for the friends Hans Christian and Georg to meet for a drink. And being the sort of men they are, going out in public means a chance to dress up as if they are "floating among Orientals."

They are called, officially, Hans Christian Andersen and Georg Carstensen; but really, they could be called Aladdin1 and Aladdin2. Here is Georg, looking princely in his fashionable Parisian outfit. Like a true Aladdin with a magic lamp to provide for him, he drinks only one glass out of every champagne bottle. He smokes only a fourth of each Cuban cigar. As for gloves, he wears a new pair every day. If he were less confident, his antics would seem like affectation. But he carries it off—everything he does tells the yokels around him about the glamor of faraway places.

Aladdin2, Hans Christian, is more modest in his spending habits and his taste for luxury. He did not have a father in diplomatic service like Georg. But though he rarely speaks well of his childhood in dingy Odense, he has not forgotten that bookshelf over his father's workbench. The books took him traveling first; they started his lifelong affair with travel. "To travel is to live," he learned to say; and to prove it, he would spend almost fifteen years of his life in other countries. But he didn't really need to go to some fantastic country to be Aladdin; in his heart of hearts he knew he was Aladdin already. He, too, was a self-made man. He had risen, with hard work and an imagination that made up fantastic tales, from provincial obscurity to fame in big cities. His life is the real fairy tale, though he is called Hans Christian and not Aladdin.

The two friends have a lot to talk about. The year before, Hans Christian built a literary bazaar. He began his new travelogue, *A Poet's Bazaar*, with a suitable epigraph:

> *Between Copenhagen and the Orient*
> *Lies the bazaar, that you are looking at here.*
> *Come, let us walk, if only on print,*
> *Through six arcades erected with a wealth of pictures.*[2]

As for Georg—he has always thought big. It is not enough to travel; you have to bring something home, too. Algiers, Morocco, Spain, North America, England, Portugal, and most of all, France—all his journeys have taught him to come home with evidence of his intimacy with other places. Not just souvenirs, though he has plenty of those. He has the heavy brocade curtains that turn his room into a richly hued tent; he has his hand-knitted Persian blankets covering every inch of the floor; his tablecloths decorated with arabesques; his divans, his ottomans, his sofas, his Moroccan pillows.

But it wasn't enough to be an eastern pasha, recently arrived from Paris, in private. He had to go out into the city, build his own "Oriental colony," and entice the public to come and admire it. Georg has a clear idea of what a Danish Orient should be: it has to be the Orient of "the child, the fairy tale book, the thousand and one nights, half Persian, half Copenhagener."[3] The atmosphere has to be dreamlike; it has to reek of fantasy and poetry; and, floating in this dream, there should be ghosts, lamps, rings, diamonds, sapphires. These would make the common man feel uncommon, while taking care of profit.

The bazaar he has built would let every Copenhagener experience the fantastic for the price of a ticket to the Tivoli Gardens.

Georg tells Hans Christian about his encounter with Christian VIII—how he convinced the king to give him fifteen acres on the outskirts of the city for 945 kroner a year. "I told him," Georg smirks, "that when the people are amusing themselves, they do not think about politics."[4]

Georg's boastfulness is understandable. Amusement has been serious business in the Tivoli from the opening season—which included a Turkish-style concert hall, bandstands, cafés, pavilions, flower gardens, mechanical amusement rides, a theater decorated in Moorish style, a Chinese bazaar, gondolas on the lake decorated with oriental lamps, even a stuffed crocodile inside an Egyptian temple. On special evenings, the fireworks on display lit up the lake. Tivoli's imaginary Orient has already become so much a part of the city that Georg can now say, "Tivoli will never be finished."

* * *

As Hans Christian walks home from the café, the street is empty; he is alone; he pulls the fez off his head. He remembers that one of his successes, a tale that has brought him fame, is only a failed love letter. He recalls this with fresh misery as if the day he heard Edvard was engaged was yesterday. Hans Christian couldn't help himself—he had rushed to Edvard and told him, "I long for you as though you were a beautiful Calabrian girl." He shivers now when he recalls Edvard's shocked, disgusted face. He sees himself slaving with ink and paper day after day, writing out his love for Edvard. He knows now that his love was always doomed, as if lover and beloved belong to two different worlds. But when it was all written, Hans Christian gave it a title, "The Little Mermaid," and he sent it to Edvard first.

Magic often confuses people; they think it is an escape from themselves and where they are. The real magic in Hans Christian's stories was that the more you traveled, the more you stayed at home and looked hard at yourself.

Hans made up a story about a mermaid who wanted to be human. This sort of story usually has three sisters, with the youngest doing everything right and being rewarded. But Hans tried something different. Not only did he spin out the tale with six sisters, all mermaid princesses. He also made the youngest, the usual heroine-elect, a strange, yearning creature who made all the wrong choices and got no reward at the end. The tale of the youngest mermaid, instead of following the usual formula of virtue or cleverness rewarded, was the tale of a tragedy queen.

Hans' little mermaid sang better than all the underwater denizens put together. When she turned fifteen, she rose above her father's palace in the watery depths and saw the world above. How strange and inviting it must have been, this colorful human town, how similar to Hans the poet's bazaar!

But the mermaid shrank the wonders of this new world to a young prince whom she saved from a shipwreck. She made a rather complicated deal with a sea witch, a deal with many conditions and clauses. The princess would exchange her mermaid's tail for a pair of beautiful legs; she would walk, even dance, but it would be terribly painful. Also, she had to let the witch cut off her tongue; she lost the power of both speech and song. She went up to the human world, gambling on a chance of making the prince love her. If she won, she would get the prince and a soul of her own. If she lost, her heart would break, and she would turn into a speck of foam on the sea.

This would later be called a child's tale, but Hans was clearly not thinking of children when he let the mermaid lose the gamble. The prince did not fall in love with her; he did not even realize he owed his life to the mermaid. He married someone else. The mermaid was given a lifeline—her sisters gave her a knife to kill him so she could grow fins again and go home. She threw away this chance, too. What could she have been thinking? What could Hans have been thinking?

Perhaps Hans remembered at this point—though he had no children—that his story had to leave behind something more than sadness. He adlibbed a new ending. The dumb girl jumped into the sea, but she rose into the air to become one of its daughters. These daughters would go to heaven in three hundred years. For every good child found by a daughter of the air, a year would be subtracted from the three hundred; for every naughty child, a year added.

Quite rightly, no one remembers this ending. The mermaid remains a mermaid, except she lives out the three hundred years of her allotted life on the seashore, in the presence of curious humans called tourists. If Hans Christian could have joined me in Copenhagen in 2012, he would have seen that his fantastic other, the little mermaid, is now part of another tale.

* * *

Once upon a time, a city that knows both fairy tales and business opportunities adopted three daughters. All three happen to be mute, and all three happen to be naked mermaids; though the youngest has legs, not fins.

The first daughter is Hans' mermaid, but she has changed from flesh to stone, not flesh to air. The city got her from a brewer, Carl Jacobsen, in 1913. The mermaid's face looks like the face of a ballerina called Ellen; her body is borrowed from a sculptor's wife, Eline. She looks cold and young, a girl who will never be a woman, though she will turn one hundred in August 2013. She has two hundred years to go before stone tries to turn to sea foam. Meanwhile she has seen a lot of humans at the Copenhagen harbor, princes and many others, come and go.

This little mermaid is in business as one of the city's official attractions. No one asked her about the terms of the contract, given the advantages of negotiating with mute girls of stone. She is a brand who needs no name; just "little mermaid" works. She *is* little—just one and a quarter meters, or four feet, high. Not only is she small; there is something modest about her, though her bronze breasts are bare. She is naked but not sexy. Her body faces the shore but she prefers to keep her head turned, facing the sea.

The day I saw her (and I suspect most days) she was turning green here and there, and she was wet and weepy. Perhaps she weeps for more than legs, prince, soul, home. Twice she has lost her head. Once her arm was sawn off. Holes were blasted in her wrist and knee. Less dire, she has had paint poured on her; a dildo attached to her hand; a burqa draped on her. Whatever the nature of assault, she has been repaired each time by her mother-city, restored to her place by the water to welcome travelers to the harbor.

But too many travelers have found this mermaid unimpressive. She really is too small; almost insignificant. Hence the need for a second daughter, the big mermaid made in China, gifted to the city in 2007 by the owner of a café at Langeliniekaj.

The big mermaid—four meters high and fourteen tons heavy—is not just big; she is positively Amazonian. She stands safely on land, on the port-of-call cruise-ship dock, leaning against a podium as if she is about to give a thank-you speech at the Oscars. The rumor is that the big mermaid looks like the café owner's niece. But for those who have not seen this niece, one look at the big mermaid's granite derriere gives her a name: J Lo. The ripe breasts could belong to an unnamed goddess of the Hindu pantheon. The belly button pierces a flat stretch of stomach.

Like many second daughters, the big mermaid makes no bones about competing with her elder sister, that weepy little bore. The granite mermaid shows off everything she has. It's a pity tails are not as sexy as legs, but she drapes her tail enticingly round the base of the podium. Her face remains vacuous as if she is afraid expression may give her wrinkles. Besides, the point of this mermaid is her body, not her face.

The third sister, as we know, is always the critical component of the trio: she is the truthful surprise in the package. The third mermaid was made of bronze by Bjørn Nørgaard in 2006 and given to the city. She lives in a new square by one of the old warehouses in the harbor, a few hundred meters from the little mermaid.

The youngest mermaid is a mutant. She is deformed; and she is in frank pain. She has legs, but all her joints show. Her hands are stuck to a rock like misshapen limpets. Her feet face outward. Her breasts hang dolefully like little papayas that refuse to ripen. But luckily she does not live alone. She lives in a water basin on its own small island; around her is a paradise that is not empty. Paradise has a Madonna nine meters high, surrounded by Adam, Christ, Maria Magdalena, Eve, The Tripartite Capital, and the Pregnant Man.

The three mermaid sisters are honored residents of the city though they remain close to the shore. It helps that they are strange; strange as they are, it helps that they are made of stone. Elsewhere is so much better in stone or in fantasy. But what if these creatures from other worlds take on flesh and blood? What if they shed mermaidhood, become human, acquire voices and rights, and become *Danish*?

WHEN ELSEWHERE COMES TO STAY: AARHUS 2012, 2005

I took a comfortable train from Copenhagen to Aarhus, which is on the east side of the peninsula of Jutland. Aarhus, the second-largest city in Denmark, is also its principal port. I liked the word Aros, and its meaning, the mouth of the river. From what I had read and heard, I got the impression that travel was essential to Aarhus. Travel was necessary for a history of trade and commerce and exploration; and its occasional corollaries, conquest, plunder, and loot. I was told to look for the Viking exhibit in the basement of a bank—the place where the remains of a Viking settlement were found. But the Vikings seem to live with greater force in the imagination of outsiders; the Aarhus I found was more preoccupied with some very different travelers—the sort who had come to stay.

On the train, a young couple who sat across watched me for a while before the woman leaned forward and asked if I was from India. I confessed that I was, and the woman pointed at her suitcase and exclaimed with triumph: "We are on our way home from the airport. We have just got back from India." Ah.

No wonder she was wearing the standard long silver earrings, the requisite number of bangles, and the regulation harem pants. The inevitable conversation about India followed, but I was more interested in Aarhus. These friendly young travelers, newly returned from a fortnight in India and trying to understand what they had seen, were among the first Aarhusians I met.

The man ran a car-repair place; the woman cooked in a school kitchen. They had lived in Aarhus all their lives. Pleased that I was so curious, they went on to describe their city. How had it changed over the years? I hadn't asked about immigrants in particular, but the answers involved frequent references to Muslims. The word Muslim was used to cover all kinds of "other" people, regardless of language or place of origin; and regardless of whether they were refugees, immigrants, or "guest workers."

In the seventies these guest workers came from Turkey, Pakistan, Morocco, and the former Yugoslavia. In the eighties and nineties came refugees and asylum seekers from Iran, Iraq, Somalia, and Bosnia. Today "the Muslims" form a very mixed minority—they have come to Denmark from more than fifty different countries.

Aarhus, with its river's mouth wide open, has seen tiny chunks of elsewhere come to its shores, become part of it.

The woman on the train said to me, "They want a mosque now. I don't think they will get it."

"Why?" I asked her.

"We are not used to noise like that," she said.

I could hear the university teacher I met in Copenhagen telling me: "We had a gallant record—we had an underground network that took thousands of Jews on fishing vessels from Denmark to safety in Sweden. Even in the seventies, there was a policy that welcomed outsiders and newcomers. All that's changed now."

I could hear the teacher's English grow more Danish in her agitation. I leaned forward encouragingly, but she was unstoppable anyway. "Now we have language and civics tests for newcomers; and citizenship contracts. We make family reunions as difficult as possible. Any citizen of non-Danish origin can be deported if he commits a crime. We don't deport other citizens when they commit crimes, do we? We send them to jail."

This anti-Muslim feeling in a country that prides itself on a tolerant historical record, and on secular, democratic, "enlightened" values, puzzled me. I dug out the facts. One estimate I found said there are about 200,000 Muslims in Denmark, out of a total population of five and a half million. About 30,000 of these report themselves as practicing Muslims—that is, they pray regularly, attend a mosque (a makeshift one or a prayer room), or see a confessional imam.[5] Why then this fear that "Danish culture" will be taken over by "Muslim culture"? Could the anti-immigrant rhetoric and the frequent references to "Danish values" have something to do with an overdose of homogeneity? The sort of nationalism that congeals into fear, anxiety, and suspicion?

All these questions reared their heads in 2005 when the largest-selling newspaper in Denmark, Aarhus-based *Morgenavisen Jyllands-Posten*, generated what has come to be called "the Muhammad cartoon crisis." (Among Muslims and some others it is called "the *Jyllands-Posten* crisis," since they do not think the crisis was about Muhammad at all.)

Jyllands-Posten published twelve cartoons on September 30, 2005. The cartoons featured Muhammad, and were sharply satirical of Muslims and Islam. They illustrated an article, "The Face of Muhammad," by the cultural editor of the paper, Flemming Rose. Rose wrote about the paper's attempt to test what he called a "creeping self-censorship" among Danish cartoonists because of the fear of Muslim fundamentalists. The apparent provocation was that the author of a children's book on the Koran and the life of the prophet had trouble getting artists to illustrate his book. The paper solicited contributions from the members of the Danish cartoonist union, the ostensible point being a debate on Islam, self-censorship and freedom of expression.

Whether they believed that Muhammad should not be depicted, or whether they objected to the provocative nature of the cartoons, the Muslims in Denmark reacted with a combination of anger and hurt. To add to the discord mix, the Danish prime minister refused to meet eleven concerned ambassadors about growing anti-Islamic rhetoric in public discourse.

The conflict between the "Danish Danes" and the "Muslim Danes" became couched in black and white, a "war of culture" waged between the democratic, rational, modern, and even "post-cultural," whatever that may be; and "un-enlightened beings" guided by "easily ignited tempers" and "ignorant people" with a "democratic deficit."[6]

But was it really so simple? Was it just about free speech?

Nuanced positions do not make good copy. Just as all Muslims became one undifferentiated body, so, conveniently, did the "indigenous" Danes. The many voices that criticizeed the "official" position or the loudest discourse got muffled. But they were there, and they spoke and wrote.

The Danish musician Kiku Day, for instance, wrote in the *Guardian*: "We were a liberal and tolerant people until the 1990s, when we suddenly awoke to find that for the first time in our history we had a significant minority group living among us. Confronted with the terrifying novelty of being a multicultural country, Denmark took a step not merely to the right but to the far right."[7] Others argued that freedom of speech is not absolute, that it has reasonable limits addressed by laws on libel, defamation and hate speech. They asked how the *Jyllands-Posten* position could help people who already feel powerless to "integrate" themselves into the larger democratic space.

Can the cartoons be considered hate speech? Do they target all Muslims by identifying them with terrorism and a barbaric culture?

An anthropologist, Peter Hervik, who teaches "migration studies," says an "incomplete narrative" has dominated public discussion on the cartoons. The narrative, in which *Jyllands-Posten* and the Danish government are innocent victims in a dispute over freedom of speech, leaves out many things. The voices of ordinary Muslims are missing in the media; and there has been a slew of negative coverage of Islam and the Muslim minority.

Hervik digs into *Jyllands-Posten*'s stories on the tried and tested theme of immigrants as a problem, and comes up with several nuggets. Just a couple of these are enough to show that the newspaper's culture war began well before the cartoons were published.

In 1997, *Jyllands-Posten* ran a story about a Danish Muslim boy, Amin. Ten-year-old Amin was expelled from a private school in Frederikssund because he refused to bathe with his Danish schoolmates. The early headlines included "School Accused of Racism." In response, *Jyllands-Posten* reasoned that Amin was expelled because he refused to integrate; he insisted on his difference. Soon the story shifted shape: it was now about what an unwashed body could do to Danish swimming pools. "The water in the pools came to serve as a metaphor of Danishness; the unwashed body would infect the water as foreignness would infect Danish cultural values."[8]

In numerous editorials and articles since, *Jyllands-Posten* has constructed the face and figure of an enemy. Some words are frequently called upon to do this: abomination (*vederstyggelig*), darkening (*formørkelse*), and "Middle Ages-like" (*middelalderlig*). Danish values are modern—open-minded, rational, extrovert; Muslims are evil and live in the Middle Ages, happy with "Afghani conditions." They do not want to integrate, though they have learned, "from home," the words *demands*, *rights* and *social welfare*. An article in 2001 in *Jyllands-Posten* called "The New Denmark" described this enemy; the article was accompanied by an image of a veiled Muslim woman.

The newspaper was not alone in its campaign over the years. The anti-Muslim rhetoric has also come from politicians and those in government. After he won the parliamentary election in November 2001, Danish Prime Minister Rasmussen launched a political strategy later referred to as "culture war" (*kulturkamp*). In 2002, the Board for Ethnic Equality was abolished. In 2005, Minister for Culture Brian Mikkelsen warned that "contemporary Muslim culture is evolving in Denmark with medieval norms and anti-democratic ways of thinking." The Conservative People's Party's Lene Espersen, who became Minister of Justice in 2001, insisted that "national values" must overcome difference: "We must hold on to Denmark as a nation-state and those values that bond us together... if people have a different ethnic background... they only need to understand the Danish culture, language and religion."[9] The Liberal Party's Birthe Rønn Hornbech, who became Minister of Integration in 2007, said in 2001: "If this tendency goes on, our country will be battered."[10] Jytte Andersen of the Social Democratic Party summed it up: "No Islamic teaching shall decide what Denmark is going to look like."[11] In 2011, the government established a "value commission" to examine what values are important for Danes.

It seems the voices of the others—those who are not fundamentalist, those who just want to get ahead with the business of living—can only be heard if they are sought out, "researched," and recorded. One such exercise found that many young Muslims are unable to identify with the old diminishing religious identity being imposed on them. "They see themselves as Danish, ethnic, Muslims, and not potential terrorists."[12]

* * *

On my way to Aarhus station, the clock struck noon. I wasn't wearing a watch, but I knew the time. The cathedral bells clanged forcefully. For someone not used to church bells ringing, and certainly not so loudly, the sound froze me for an instant. But I knew it wasn't noise; it was the ringing of bells. I wondered then if the woman from the train to Aarhus may say the same thing if she, too, could learn what an *azan* ringing out from a mosque sounds like. Would she then acknowledge that it was strange sometimes, but not exactly noise?

Months later, far from Aarhus and Denmark, I went back to these places via email. Waiting in my inbox was one of those titbits from the net that friends these days feel compelled to send each other. Reliable or not, some of these titbits are eloquent. This one told me that Danish parents must pick a name from an approved list of seven thousand, most of which are West European and English names. Recently, a few non-European names, such as Ali and Hassan, have been added to accommodate immigrants.[13] The list did not include either Alauddin or Aladdin, though. I wonder what our old friends, Georg and Hans Christian, would have to say about that.

9

SEEING PALESTINE

SEEING PALESTINE, 1819 TO 2013

It was my last day in Ramallah. To my great fortune, I spent much of the day in conversation with a Palestinian well placed to put in perspective everything I had seen and heard in the occupied West Bank. Raja Shehadeh is a lawyer, and knows, firsthand, the ways in which the land has been "held hostage to various views" and remapped. Raja is also a writer, and a walker. Because he is a walker, the land is not something abstract for him. He has made it his business to know every wildflower and weed, every spring and stone ruin he comes across in his wanderings in the hills and valleys of Palestine.

Seeing Palestine—what is *seen* in Palestine—has, for hundreds of years, depended on what the beholders are looking for; on the burden of their beliefs, the depth of their wishes to map the place afresh, the sweep of their imagination. Given the variety of beholders, Palestine has been invented time and again. Most of these inventions have been exercises in imposing a sacred landscape on a real one. The holy land and the holy book have been read together: "Palestine is one vast table whereupon God's messages to men have been drawn, and graven deep in living characters by the Great Publisher."[1]

My new friend Raja Shehadeh is perfectly aware of what it is to see a place and imbue it with multiple meanings. "The Western world's confrontation with Palestine is perhaps the longest running drama in history," he wrote in his extraordinary book on a vanishing landscape, *Palestinian Walks*.

Several moments of this drama have been recorded in travelers' accounts. One of these, by Edward Robinson in 1833, reported how biblical places and persons came to life before his eyes. He wrote of

> the city where God of old had dwelt, and where the Savior of the world had lived and taught and died. From the earliest childhood I had read of and studied the localities of this sacred spot; now I beheld them with my own eyes; and they all seemed familiar to me, as if the realization of a former dream. I seemed to be again among cherished scenes of childhood, long unvisited, indeed, but distinctly recollected.[2]

Robinson experienced an overwhelming sense of connection, of "coming home." He would not be the last to go through this epiphany; but there were others who had to work harder to draw such a moment out of Palestine.

Other nineteenth-century visitors, many of them Protestant Europeans and Americans immersed in the Bible, experienced a disconnect—between the "the land of milk and honey," the divine landscape of their expectations, and the disappointingly real land before them. This was especially true of Jerusalem, always of profound symbolic value. Instead of the "shining city on a hill" the travelers saw a dusty, provincial outpost. Luckily, reality was not necessarily a deterrent. When he was in Palestine in 1869, wrote the Reverend Andrew Thomson, he was conducted by his guide to an open spot covered with large stones. On learning that this banal spot was Jacob's well, Thomson confessed to "a temporary feeling of extreme disappointment." But he was also certain that "On this very spot Jesus had sat and conversed. From this very point he had looked forth on the scenes on which we were now looking." The problem was that he was "not prepared for such a complete defacement of the old picture as this."

Like most visitors to the Holy Land, Reverend Thomson expected to see things pretty much as Jesus and his disciples had left them. What exactly did that mean? Most travelers wanted real-life versions of the pictures they had seen in the illustrated Bibles of their childhood. When this did not happen, they were disappointed; but, like a miracle, their letdown could also turn to certainty. This *had* to be evidence of defacement. Sacred scenes and places defaced: this called for a mission, a sacred mission, to restore what had been damaged or lost.

In 2013, as we sat in his spring-beautiful garden, Raja Shehadeh told me: "Interpreting a religious text as real history, as real geography, is sacrilegious as far as I am concerned."

It is not as if all travelers shared the zealous enthusiasm of the evangelicals. Mark Twain, part of a tourist excursion organized by the Plymouth Church, wrote of a "peculiar knobby city"—the knobs being the domes on the rooftops of Jerusalem. As for the land, he found it "dismal," "barren," and "unpicturesque."

"It is," he concluded, "a hopeless, dreary, heartbroken land." Herman Melville agreed. "No country will more quickly dissipate romantic expectation than Palestine—particularly Jerusalem," Melville wrote in his journal. Twain and Melville were, like others, bothered by the gap between imagination and lived reality; but both were too skeptical of missionary proclivities to trade immediate disappointment for immediate reinvention. Melville, for example, recorded his encounters with American missionaries, "preparing the soil literally and figuratively" for Jewish restoration to the Holy Land. He regarded Christian Zionism, which was an obsession among evangelicals, as a "preposterous Jew mania" that was "half melancholy, half farcical." As for the assorted "creeds" who came to see and "make" the holy land, whether Presbyterians, Baptists, Catholics, Methodists or Episcopalians, "they entered the country with their verdicts already prepared, and they could no more write dispassionately and impartially about it than they could about their own wives and children."[3]

From once-in-a-lifetime package tours to "vicarious journeys of the imagination," nineteenth-century travel through "biblical lands" evoked in the traveler a combination of wonder, delight, and disappointment. These were recorded in more than words. The nascent medium of photography and the advent of archeology influenced how the Holy Land was seen. Photographs of biblical sites replaced fanciful illustrations based on artists' sketches — but the medium that promised truth and accuracy could also produce distorted views. The subjects sought out were those that would confirm connections to stories from the Bible. If the images included people, they had to be doing something suitably biblical or "antique," say a man tending his flock or a woman drawing water from a well. The scene had to evoke scripture. In a photograph entitled "Jews at the Western Wall," for example, French photographer Felix Bonfils showed a group of Jews huddled by the Wailing Wall, praying. In 1854, his compatriot, artist and archaeologist Auguste Salzmann, produced photographs that used light and form to animate old buildings in Jerusalem. The idea was to record monuments left by the Crusades, and find evidence of the biblical kingdom of David for the controversial historical and architectural theories of scholar Félicien de Saulcy. Salzmann's photographs, said de Saulcy, were "brute, conclusive facts."[4]

Western travelers saw Palestine as a biblical landscape, as arid and desolate, as awe-inspiring, as a home promised by God. So overwhelming was the demand of both real and imaginary land to be seen and explained, that many managed not to see, or barely see, the people.

Years later, this may have helped see Palestine as a land that needed people, especially the sort of people who needed a home. To superimpose a new map on an existing one, it was not enough to conjure a landscape of belief, and people it with extracts from religious texts. The place was important for international geopolitics; but military and economic aims could coexist with religious fervor. Western European powers were poised to intervene if Ottoman rule in the region collapsed; they saw clearly the major trade routes to India; and, with the completion of the Suez Canal connecting the Mediterranean and Red Seas, the area grew even more vital. The question then, and in 1948, when a new nation was mapped onto the land, was what to do with the people already there. The question blurred in some heads, so when it was asked again, it became: But were there people?

One apologist for Eretz Israel writes of "a land virtually laid waste with little population." One historian after another, goes the claim, has shown that "in the twelve and a half centuries between the Arab conquest in the seventh century and the beginnings of the Jewish return in the 1880's, Palestine was laid waste." The fertile land described in the Bible had "vanished into desert and desolation," and, in the mid-eighteenth century, Palestine did not have enough people to till its soil. Not surprisingly, "the British Consul in Palestine reported in 1857 that 'The country is in a considerable degree empty of inhabitants and *therefore its greatest need is that of a body of population.*'"[5]

And years later, Golda Meir would announce, "There are no Palestinians."

No natives, or not enough of them; transients or nomads, certainly not a "nation"; then from there, "Arabs," the word sounding a little like "imposters," living on the land that belongs to the Jewish people, only they have been away for three thousand years and are now back home.

What is it like to be told you and your family don't exist, or that what was home in a people's living memory was not actually their home at all? Edward Said took statements like Golda Meir's and transformed them into questions Palestinians could ask after their existence had been overlooked or denied, or their existence was noticed long enough to dispossess them, or send them into exile or to refugee camps. "Do we exist?" asks Said. "What proof do we have? The further we get from the Palestine of our past, the more precarious our status, the more disrupted our being, the more intermittent our presence."[6]

* * *

In 2013, I went to Palestine with the heavy baggage of half-knowledge, conscious I was following in the steps of a long trail of travelers, and, like some of them, determined to acquit myself with honor.

The Holy Land is really a small place. But it seems open, an endless series of gentle low hills that descend to the sea on one side, the desert on the other. There are lush valleys and silvery olive trees everywhere. I was not prepared for the beauty of the land. But beautiful places, especially those called holy, are doomed to invite trouble. Seeing Palestine, it is easy to see there's trouble, great trouble, in the Holy Land.

But I was not in Palestine to see a holy land. (Living in India, it is easy to develop an allergy to pilgrims of the spirit.) Friends in the university arranged for me to meet writers, academics, students, activists. I was also able to join a tour organized by a Palestinian activist I had met on his visit to India. These tours are specially organized by the activists for international delegations and individuals, and for Palestinians from '48 Palestine—what is now Israel. Every day, a group of us was driven past checkpoints, on smooth settler roads or potholed Palestinian roads, to see what was called, in earlier times, "brute, conclusive facts." Or, in the more recent phrase Israel uses like a tic, *facts on the ground.*

FACTS ON THE GROUND, PEOPLE ON THE GROUND: OCCUPIED PALESTINE, 2013

Facts on the ground—Israel has plenty of these. In fact, the state of Israel seems to exist only to build facts on the ground then flaunt them. This was evident the day I arrived in Tel Aviv and made my way to Occupied Ramallah. Over the days that followed, I saw and heard more of these facts in Nablus, Jerusalem, Bethlehem, Hebron; and in the villages between these cities, some of them nestling in a curve of hills.

The facts are solid. It is hard to argue with facts made of steel, concrete, or stone. The Israeli settlements sit on hilltops, kings of all they survey. They were easy to identify—the prefabricated units look alike. And there were so many of them, whichever window I looked out of, whichever road I took, whichever hill I climbed or valley I went down, that I felt I was inside the Matrix. These units were cloning themselves like Mr. Smith. The settlements were eating up the land, bite after large bite. They were cutting into and gouging out hills; they had dislocated villages that had been there as long as people can remember. They had stolen springs, uprooted venerable olive trees. They had demolished houses. They had destroyed the lives of the people who lived there, their work, their community life, their memories of the past, and their hopes for the future.

I saw these facts over and over again. In Beit El, Ariel, Benyamin, Har Gilo, Alkana, Ma'ale Adumin, Ma'ale Lavona, more Ma'ales than I can remember—settlements with Judaized names of old places, often referring to their hilltop location.

Not all the settlements need the expanse of hills. In Jerusalem, the strategy is to take over the city house by house. In East Jerusalem, I saw, for the first time, what rooftop colonization looks like. If the Palestinians in the building resist intimidation or money, the Israeli settler can take over the rooftop with a prefab house, fly an Israeli flag like a signpost, and commute across rooftops made secure with Israeli guard-cabins and surveillance cameras. The rooftops have been fixed, a friend from Jerusalem told me wryly, so the settlers can walk or cycle across the rooftops "without having to see an Arab."

In Hebron, the settlement tactic is "slicing." I saw the old market, commercial heart of Hebron, in shreds. The functioning part is covered with netting; the settlers above throw their refuse on this net. To one side of the market, I looked up and saw some settler children playing. One of them, a little girl with curly hair, saw me looking. Before my lips could stretch into a smile, she turned around, bent over, pointed at her bottom mockingly. Contempt seeps easily into the cement and the blood of the settlements, even the youngest of blood.

In the ghost-town part of Hebron Market, three Palestinian children sat bent over their laptops, one modem among them. I climbed the pitch-dark stairway to the houses above a sealed shop. The terrace opened onto a congested world of rooftops, cheek by jowl. I was shown the holes on the silvery water tank on the terrace; I was told they were made by the settler family next door. I was told how easy it is for settlers to walk from one rooftop to another, harass residents.

Hilltops, rooftops, markets, water, land and more land have been grabbed; more is in the process of being grabbed. Israel is the only nuclear power in the region. It has the fourth-strongest army in the world. It has the consistent backing of the preeminent military power, the US. But still, the settlements and settlers have to be *protected*. Security is the most important word in Israel. So the next set of hard facts on the ground: checkpoints, watchtowers, barricades; electrified fences; loops of barbed wire; army-only roads; an entire network of roads connecting settlements, to keep settlers safe from the Palestinians who have to use bypasses, tunnels, and circuitous routes that turn a fifteen-minute trip to an hour's bumpy ride. And the Wall: a "separation barrier" now cuts up the West Bank, walls in more land for Israel, walls in more people in Palestine.

If these are Israel's facts on the ground, Palestine, too, has some facts on the ground. Except these facts live and breathe because they are *people* on the ground. Khalid. Abu Nidal. Omar. Muneer.

When I met Khalid and Abu Nidal, farmers in the West Bank, the Palestinian friends who had arranged the "alternative tour" sent along an interpreter, a young woman in blue jeans and a red-and white-checked shirt. She had a long pale face with strong eyebrows and full rose-pink lips: a Palestinian Madonna. Her head was framed by a white scarf; a sliver of dark brown fabric high on the forehead showed what was holding her hair in place under the scarf. She grew up in London but chose to return to Palestine as an adult. "I am the only Welsh-born Palestinian you will meet," she laughed.

The day was clear and sunny, perfect for a road trip. A day out in the country, but in an occupied land. What this meant was that new sights and new friendships could never be separated from sadness. To leave Ramallah we had to go past the Qalandia checkpoint. As I pulled out my passport, my eyes met those of the young Israeli guard manning the checkpoint. A boy, a mere boy, with loaded guns. His face was expressionless as he waved us on.

The West Bank is small; for an Indian, it is tiny. In what seemed like no time at all, we were at our destination, Al-Laban or Lubban Village, twenty kilometers south of the city of Nablus. The hilltop settlements of Ma'ale Levona, Eli and Shilo surround the village from above. Ma'ale Levona—the name is the judaized version of Lubban—was established by Hanan Porat, a prominent member of the Gush Emunim. The Gush Emunim, or "Block of the Faithful," is an umbrella organization of Zionists; their central slogan can be summed up as "the Land of Israel for the People of Israel, According to the Torah of Israel." They are committed to establishing Jewish settlements in the West Bank, the Gaza Strip, and the Golan Heights for ideological reasons. They do not need the cover of the usual security reason; for them, the West Bank heartland is promised Biblical land, Judea and Samaria.[7] And they know how to wield a powerful political weapon—the "creation of facts in the field."

In what became Ma'ale Levona, "temporary" caravans were first placed as an "outpost" on land expropriated from the villages. These caravans were, over time, replaced by fancy villas.

Eli was established in 1984 on Ali hilltop—and the name Ali judaized to Eli. Mobile caravans were added over a period of time, and the settlement grew till it occupied seven hilltops belonging to Palestinian villages, including Lubban.

In 2005, Israeli occupation forces surrounded the colony with a "security belt" to provide "protection" for Eli. More land was confiscated from Lubban Village. When the settlement's wastewater treatment plant became dysfunctional, the wastewater was dumped on the lands of Lubban Village, destroying crops. The settlers regularly attack the villagers, especially during the olive-harvest season.

* * *

The car pulled over by two other cars waiting for us. Three couples with children got out of the cars. They, like me, were being taken to Lubban to meet one farmer's family. But we were different sorts of visitors. They were Palestinians from '48 Palestine, what is now Israel. The three Palestinian couples had brought their children along; the children were seeing the West Bank for the first time. I wish I had asked the adults how they felt, being taken on a tour of the West Bank. Instead I watched the children giving themselves to uninhibited enjoyment.

We made our way to the house of a farmer, Khalid Samih Hammed Draghmeh, also known as Abu Jamal, or Father of Jamal. Khalid's house, and what remained of his fields, were cut off from the rest of Lubban Village.

The first thing we saw as we walked toward Khalid's house was that the driveway was blocked with stones to keep the settlers away. The house was an old *khan*—a roadside inn or caravanserai. When we admired the main door of the khan, Khalid said it was a replacement. The old door was beautiful, but the settlers took it away.

The old khan is in the way. If the settlement of Ma'ale Levona is to be linked to other settlements, extending from the Jordan Valley to the Green Line, the khan cannot remain as it is: Palestinian. In 2003, the settlers began to attack the khan; in 2007 they managed to occupy it. They built a kitchen; set up a portable toilet; flew an Israeli flag over the house. They began to hold events, including religious rituals, in the house. The settlers were there for three months. Khalid filed papers in the occupation court to prove he owned the khan and the land around it. "But that was not enough," said Khalid. "They left because we, the real owners, did not leave them alone."

I looked at him, this wiry straight-backed man, trying to read between his lines. His lined face was crowned by flying curly hair, a hint of red in it. His mustache, too, was the same color; on his chin the stubble was gray. His gray nylon jacket had cheerful white stripes and a red patch that said *Motorcycle*. One of the visitors aimed a camera at Khalid and he froze, a grin bringing out a surprisingly deep dimple on a weather-beaten cheek. The photo taken, he came back to life.

"There is another reason the settlers want the house and the land around it," Khalid said, gesturing for us to follow him. He took us to one side of the house and showed us a small tank by what used to be a spring and a well. The tank looked like a meaningless empty pit, a zoo cage in the open with no animal in it. An old tire lay to one side among the weeds.

Many Zionists believe that Moses once washed himself in this tank. The settlers above the village, as well as some Zionists from elsewhere, used to come here and wash themselves, said Khalid, "to absolve themselves of their sins." One day, said Khalid with a kind of stern glee, he locked them in. Then he emptied the tank of water. But still, "They badger me to give them the house and tank because they think it is their history. I said I would if they gave us Jerusalem." The small triumph of words, the not-so-small force they carry.

But the settlers from Ma'ale Levona did not give up after leaving the khan. Sometimes they offered Khalid money, sometimes "joint ventures." Sometimes they sent people, from intelligence officers to rabbis, to pressure him to abandon or sell the land. When none of this worked, the tactics grew more direct. The settlers demolished the walls Khalid had built on his land; they uprooted his trees; they killed his horse. Khalid was arrested six times. He got "notifications" from the Israeli army to leave the khan in 2004, 2006, 2009, and 2010.

Once, when Khalid was not home, about thirty-five settlers came down with sticks and pipes. They beat up his young sons, Jamal, Mohmin, and Noor. His wife, Umm Jamal, was stuck alone inside the house, not knowing what to do.

The group of visitors fell silent. What further questions could we ask?

Khalid went into the house and emerged with the papers to the land and the khan. As we looked at the neatly colored maps he must have shown many times before, Khalid broke the silence among us. The settlement is a daily threat to his house, his land, and the family's safety, said Khalid, but he has not given up either. He blocks the driveway with stones over and over again, he said. He takes down the sign that this is a resort stop for Israelis every time it is put up. He keeps the "Moses tank" empty. He cultivates what remains of his land. Volunteers from Palestinian and international groups help him with farm work every two weeks.

All talk of settlers and struggles was forgotten as we ate lunch together. The group from '48 Palestine unpacked a simple but delicious picnic lunch, complete with cake. Khalid contributed fresh fruit and a salad of farm-fresh vegetables. The children from '48 Palestine ran around exploring a Palestine they had only heard about before. One of them, a little boy, crawled up every tree trunk he could manage; his T-shirt was smeared with mud from the land he was conquering inch by inch.

After lunch, Khalid took us around what remained of his land. He showed us the hills that used to belong to him and his family. He pointed to the hills—where Eli is—and said, "They stole two springs." We saw the old olive press, locked up and no longer used, mute testimony to the loss of livelihood. But Khalid was not going to let us go on this melancholy note. He went into the fields and returned with juicy pears, fat lemons, thick and succulent mint: parting presents. Our bags and hands were full as we walked down the driveway to the cars. "I'm not going to leave my house or my land," Khalid called after us.

We drove down the road, westward, past hill and settlement, valleys and gates. We were on our way to meet another farmer, in a village called Mas'ha.

FATHERING STRUGGLE: ABU NIDAL

He was a stocky, well-built farmer, the fifty-five-year-old man with the starched white lacy cap who met us at the first of several gates. We already knew that most of his land was gone; his family had been living in siege for years. But I could see nothing helpless about him, nothing that evoked pity. He was poised, articulate. Everything about him said he *knew* this land. He was where he should be; he was at home.

The man's name is Hani Amer, but his eldest son is called Nidal, or struggle. So he is Abu, father of, Nidal. His wife, Monira Amer, is Umm Nidal. (I came across any number of Abu Nidals and Umm Nidals in Palestine.) This Abu Nidal lives in Mas'ha Village. The village of Mas'ha is in Salfit District, thirty-five kilometers to the west of Nablus and six kilometers to the east of the Green Line, the trembly serrated line that marks Israel's pre-1967 border.

Mas'ha was unlike any village I had seen before; but I was told Mas'ha was not always like this, a semi-ghost village with shops closed, farmers unsure of getting to their land to water it, or to harvest their olives. The market used to be busy till it was destroyed by the Israeli army in 2000 when the Second Intifada broke out.

Abu Nidal lives in Mas'ha Village—in a manner of speaking. The house sat between the two main gates to the village. It was, in effect, separated from the village, and from the Israeli settlement nearby, by four layers of "security." One of these layers was an electrified fence. I stood outside, waiting for the yellow barricade and the fence to be opened. In those fifteen minutes of waiting, I saw more gate-fence-barricade-wall in one place than I had ever seen before. Two formidable fences enclosed the Israeli settlement protectively. And as if this did not say enough, on another side I saw a locked gate with the sign: "Mortal Danger—Military Zone. Any Person Who Passes or Damages the Fence Endangers His Life." The gates and barricades made a cage of Abu Nidal's house. But they could be opened, at least in theory, at least by the Israeli soldiers; unlike the walls.

A wall of concrete slabs twenty meters to the east of the house, the gray slabs reaching high into the air: that was wall number one. The second wall, a high wire wall on the western side, was topped with great big loops of barbed wire. Even in a land where barbed wire is ubiquitous, this was an eloquent sight. The third wall to the south surrounded the house; it had a gate that led to "the Wall's road," a military road there to "service" the wall. And there was a fourth wall from the north with a small gate next to the concrete wall. Together they surrounded the house.

This, I saw, is one face of occupation.

Abu Nidal led us to a small opening alongside the concrete wall and wire fence; this was the gate the family and their visitors had to use to go in and out. Every time the gate was opened, an alarm went to the Israeli army. Abu Nidal now had the key to this gate after years of fighting for it. He recalled what it was like before he got the key. For months after the wall was built, they were not allowed visitors at all. Coverage on Israeli TV led to an army decision that "periodic" visits should be allowed, but only those approved by the army.

Abu Nidal told us of the time his son Shaddad, then three years old, got stuck outside. The family was helpless, locked in. Friends of the family had to throw supplies over the gate for several days. Abu Nidal now had the key to the gate, but, warned by sensors on the fence-wall, the army knew when people visited him. At the entrance of this gate, by a painted flag, I saw a declaration in graffiti that Abu Nidal translated for me: This is neither Israel, nor Palestine, nor no man's land. It's Abu Nidal's.

Abu Nidal is an extraordinary man in an extraordinary situation.

He had sold his other house in the village—he had burned his bridges so he had no recourse but to live here and fight. "Our dignity comes from the land," he said. "My family has been on this land for generations." Abu Nidal's father and grandfather were farmers. Abu Nidal also described himself as a refugee from Kufr Qasim.

The village of Mas'ha is considered the "mother village" of Kufr Qasim town, which is in the "triangle" region inside the 1949 Green Line. Before the upheaval of 1948, what Palestinians remember as the Nakba, or the catastrophe, Mas'ha lands grew westward up to the fertile area near the Al Oja River. Many farmers from Mas'ha Village lived in Kufr Qasim since their farmlands were close by. After the Nakba in 1948, Mas'ha was split into two unequal parts. Seventy percent of the land was annexed by Israel, including the non-Jewish town of Kufr Qasim. Many families like that of Abu Nidal's became akin to refugees in their own village, in the thirty percent of Mas'ha that was left to the West Bank.

Then, during the Suez crisis, on October 29, 1956, Magav, Israel's border police, shot and killed forty-eight "Israeli Arabs"— or '48 Palestinians—in Kufr Qasim. They were shot as they were on their way home from work, for violating a curfew they had not been told about. Six of them were women, one of them pregnant; and twenty-three of them were children. Again, Palestinian survivors fled the town.

What had life been like for those who left Kufr Qasim? Abu Nidal gave us an idea. In 1978, the village faced an onslaught by the Gush Emunim, and more village land was confiscated for Jewish construction. Three Israeli settlements were built on Mas'ha land: Elkana, Sha'are Tikva, and Etz Efrayim. Elkana is literally at the heels of Abu Nidal's house. Abu Nidal said this settlement grew out of a military compound used by the British army, the Jordanian army, then the Israeli army. The settlers moved in around the eighties in mobile caravans, a typical ploy. The settlement grew into a colony of smart houses.

* * *

Abu Nidal told the story in his own direct way: "One day workers came to lay the foundations on the land next door," he began. His arms made large gestures, his hands emphasized the important point. "This was village land so of course we protested. They said the land is not being used, we have confiscated it. Take it to court if you want. We got a lawyer and he took the matter to Tel Aviv. But the case dragged on. There was more than enough time for houses to come up on our land, houses and gardens and swimming pools. It was all done, and then the Israeli High Court finally said Elkana was illegal. We had won."

He paused. His left arm went up, moved the lacy cap back and forth on his head as if he was itchy. "We had won—but if we wanted our land back, we had to pay for everything, all their illegally built things. Houses, pools, gardens, waterworks, electricity, Internet, telephones, everything. Do you think all our money, the money of the whole village put together, could pay for even one day of their construction in Elkana?"

Obviously Elkana remained, legal or illegal, court or no court. It did better. Mas'ha was barricaded with rocks and dirt mounds on both ends—protecting the settlement and blockading the village. It became easy for the settlers to go down a settler-only artery to the settler-only four-lane highway leading to Tel Aviv and Jerusalem.

Going around Abu Nidal's house, I could see that he, Monira and their six children shared a fence with three of the Elkana villas. I didn't see a single settler in the flesh, though given how close these villas are, maybe the family could look into the set-tlers' comfortable rooms. Maybe the settlers, too, could look into Abu Nidal's rooms, see Monira kneading bread, Abu Nidal sitting on his sofa, sipping black tea and brooding.

Since the settlement—and life with the settlers—was a fait accompli, they sold the settlers apples and apricots grown on his land, said Abu Nidal. He would sell them vegetables from his greenhouse. There was, for a time, a delicate balance of coexistence; life had to be lived, food grown, bought and sold, eaten.

Abu Nidal used to be allowed to go through the Elkana settlement to his land. The permit was for three months, but there was always a runaround. He never knew if it would work for three months, or whether he would get it again. He wasted time and money; he felt assaulted, he said. "I had to have a permit to reach my land, just meters away from where Elkana was built."

"And then—"said Abu Nidal, pausing as he looked at his house surrounded by wall, fence, wire, and settlements. We looked with him. "For the last ten years," he said, "this has been my reality." In case we didn't understand, he added, "I don't feel at peace." He covered his eyes with his hand for an instant.

* * *

Abu Nidal's current state of siege happened over the years.

In 1991, a part of Abu Nidal's house was demolished for being "too close to the asphalt." In 1994, the restaurant he owned was demolished. In 2003, the nursery and shop were confiscated—to build the wall. In 2004, the poultry farm was demolished.

In 2003, Abu Nidal told people from the Anti-Apartheid Wall Campaign, the same people who had taken us to meet him: "We cannot move whenever we want. They say the gates will open at eight or nine in the morning but they may not come before eleven. Somehow we manage to go where we need to, especially the children going to school. But if they put up the Wall from the west we will not be able to move even this much. I will not be able to go work in Kufr Qasim. I expect them to close all around the house, I know this house will be surrounded by walls. I live this reality. I don't live in America, this is my reality."[8]

Abu Nidal sighed. Ten years later, he was still living the same reality, the sigh seemed to say. Then he returned to 2003, spoke of the way the wall came up in front of his house. The modus operandi was typical: "I know the Israelis very well," he said. "I worked for them for years."

At first Abu Nidal was offered large sums of money for his property.

"There is no price for my land, my trees," said Abu Nidal to the Israeli officers trying to persuade him.

Since Abu Nidal could not be bought, an Israeli officer threatened him that a shooting could be "arranged" at the settlement. Abu Nidal could be charged for it, labeled a terrorist. His house could easily be bulldozed.

The bulldozer came as promised. One afternoon, Abu Nidal came home to find workers ready to bulldoze his yard and house. They said they were building a security fence. Abu Nidal said he told them, "I will take this rock and smash your heads."

"That man said to me," Abu Nidal told us, "the bulldozers don't care whether you have a problem or not. They just destroy everything." He fidgeted uneasily, as if the white plastic chair he was sitting on was too small for him.

The bulldozer returned, even though Palestinian, Israeli, and international activists were holding a "peace camp" in Mas'ha.

The Caterpillar bulldozer moved downhill, pushing dirt in its wake. The border police waited in their jeeps near Abu Nidal's fence, rifles in hand. The bulldozer turned round and advanced uphill. The dozer's chains clanked; its driver in the bulletproof cabin looked down from his height. The activists rushed from their tents, linked arms to make a chain round Abu Nidal's house. The dozer turned. It went about its work, scooping up land, then flattening it on both sides of the planned wall. Then the dozer turned once more, made its way purposefully toward the animal shed. The activists rushed to block it. But this time the police swung into action; forty-five of them were dragged into buses and driven to prison. The shed came down. The house remained, but on the Israeli side of the fence.

It could have been worse if the activists had not been there, Abu Nidal told us. But he also said, in the same breath, "They wanted to help. But I know how the Israelis take over the land." He shook his head. "I know there's no point expecting anything else from them." When the bulldozers came back next, they worked ruthlessly. "They finished the wall in a day."

* * *

How many times had Abu Nidal told this story in the decade that had gone by? I felt his generosity, and the pain, the sheer tedium, of having to prod that old wound every time his "case" had to be offered as a bit of evidence against the occupation.

His brother and family were now trying to work on his land. But working the land was no longer profitable. Abu Nidal was now talking about farmers' concerns, the need to survive the present. He built a well seven years ago, but "they" want to destroy that. He spoke of using diesel, which meant high running costs. The Palestinian Authority was supposed to help "rehabilitate" his situation, he said. But they backed out, saying they had no jurisdiction because of the wall. I could see Abu Nidal trying to keep his face neutral as he said this. But he could not keep it up. "Oslo was a big lie," he said sharply. "They deceived us, turned us into slaves. Till the day the accords were signed, we could fight as people whose rights were violated by the Israeli occupation. Then the accords put the Israelis on the right side. I mourned the day they signed in Oslo and made us strangers in our own land." His energy came back to him, thinking of Oslo. It made him combative again. "I will resist both the Israelis and the PA," he said.

Some of the Palestinian visitors laughed. Amid the laughter, one man, still grinning, said, "Oh, let's not talk about the PA. They are good people after all." There was more laughter; Abu Nidal looked sheepish, then joined in the laughter.

* * *

We walked around, listening to Abu Nidal. A little boy who had come with the visiting group hung from the yellow barricade, lifting his feet off the ground. He didn't call out to his parents to show off; clearly he sensed something unhappy and adult was being talked about. But still he looked smug, having got past then hung effortlessly from one of *their* gates. I turned from the boy to the Elkana settlement sitting like a solid shadow just behind

Abu Nidal's house. Elkana was part of a cluster of settlements around the huge Ariel complex and the Ariel Industrial Park inside the West Bank. The security fence made a loop into the Green Line, taking in the complex, and, almost "incidentally," a nice chunk of Palestinian land.

Abu Nidal, his wife and six sons lived in this isolated house, their resources exhausted in more ways than one by the wall. Abu Nidal was afraid for his family's safety; he was concerned about his livelihood. The settlers continued to threaten the family, pelting stones now and then, either to keep them awake at night or to scare the children when they play outside.

But this was a man who went to court and told them, "You are not a state, you are a mob." I could not imagine Abu Nidal giving up.

We shook hands; it seemed impossible to say anything more than thanks, though it was not clear what we were thanking him for. One of the group added, "We are very happy to have met a brave man."

"There's something I need to tell you," replied Abu Nidal. "All these problems I have, they are easier to handle than hearing someone praise me." We shook hands again.

I took one last look at the slabs of concrete standing firm before his house, the wall that made sure Abu Nidal could not see the valley from his house. The wall stood ugly and gray, but there was a bird painted on it, a yellow bird with pink-edged feathers. Abu Nidal's children had painted the bird with its wings open in flight.

I love this dust and this land, Abu Nidal had said over and over again. Khalid, too, had used words to this effect. We somehow expect farmers to say this, but what about shopkeepers? We drove to Hebron.

Deep in the old market in Hebron, past the stores sealed with iron, I found a checkpoint waiting for me. A sign at the checkpoint said: "This is the town of Abner. Please show respect for this sanctified site." I emerged from the dark checkpoint into the sunlight, and saw, to my left, the Ibrahimi Mosque, the old heart of an old city. This mosque is supposed to be the burial place of Abraham, Isaac and Rebecca, Joseph, Jacob and Leah. I also remembered: this is the place where one morning during the Ramzan month in 1994, a man called Baruch Goldstein, a doctor from Brooklyn who had become a settler in Hebron, opened fire on the worshipers. Before he was killed, the healer in military uniform murdered twenty-nine people who were, perhaps, trying to heal themselves with prayer.

But I didn't want to think about 1994 or Goldstein; this was 2013, and I had enough trouble understanding what I had seen of the "town of Abner" so far. I was not even going to the mosque; I wanted to see the old commercial center. We turned to the right. But before we could get to the main street, we had to pass one more obstacle. The ubiquitous prefab security cabin sat in our way, and a couple of young soldiers from the border security force stood outside it. They ignored three of us, obviously Indian, and we walked past them. But the young locals in our group, two boys and a girl, were stopped and asked why they were with foreigners. They were asked to hand over their ID cards. There was a flurried exchange; a man from the shop across the street hurried to the cabin, explained that we were visiting him. We were taken into the shop quickly.

The shopkeeper was introduced to us as Muneer. He invited us to sit, drink tea. His son arranged plastic chairs in a tight ring in the small shop, pottery and bric-a-brac all round us.

"I want to tell you about this street," Muneer began. "My father used to run a shop here and I helped him. See these photographs, see how busy it was till the year 2000." We passed around the black-and-white market photos silently. Shuhada Street was closed in 2000, and since then it has been under the Border Security Force. Muneer's seventy-five-year-old father and his friend went many times to the authorities, but nothing changed. "Open your shops," they said, "but we have control over entry to the street." Muneer still had to check with the guards before his family or friends could visit. As for customers—"I needed three people to run a shop before," he said. "Now I can run all the six open shops here myself. But I will stay. I will try to open the shop every day." He spoke quietly, with great dignity, this man. "So many journalists and delegations come here," he said. "But..." he added gently then fell silent, as if to spare us the knowledge of our impotence. I shook his hand with both my hands; I felt bad to let his hand go.

Outside Muneer's shop, Shuhada Street, the main street of the market, waited for us. Except this was a ghost street in a ghost market, with a couple of token shops open for business on principle. The road was divided; the main thoroughfare was for settlers, leaving a narrow strip for Palestinians. A settler family walked down the middle of the empty road. The man was large, bespectacled. He had with him his wife and two children. A family on an outing, the father herding them protectively: I couldn't believe how menacing the sight was.

Once the family disappeared from view, we walked on. The streets were deserted. Once I saw a childish face peeping out at me from a balcony enclosed like a cage. We reached a turning with a road sign to stop. The young Palestinians said they could not go beyond that point, but we Indians could. We turned back.

* * *

I wondered what city shopkeeper Muneer and village farmer Omar would say to each other, what notes they would compare if they ever met. We had met Omar that morning on the way to Hebron.

Omar lived in Walajeh, a hilly village outside Bethlehem that has been shrinking since 1948. Standing before his house, Omar indicated a hill across the Green Line: that was the village, he said, and everyone was expelled in 1948. Most went to refugee camps. Some moved to the hill we were standing on. Parts of this hill, the new Walajeh, were confiscated in 1967. Then, in 2006, Omar saw the Nakba for the third time. The Wall came to Walajeh. "They used two thousand tons of dynamite building the wall," said Omar. "They must have hoped my house would fall."

As I looked at the wall, it seemed to grow more forbidding by the minute. When it was done with Walajeh, the wall would encircle the village, and there would be a gate under army control. Two percent of the village land would be left to the villagers. The house that Omar refused to leave would be surrounded by an electric fence five meters away. Cameras would monitor the house. The only exit, a tunnel made just for this house, was already there. It was hard to take in, this one-house apartheid tunnel built at considerable cost, sitting before me.

Omar's work permit was revoked at the checkpoint when he was on his way home from work. The reason? Security. How would he live? "We are farmers," he said. "We can live simply, on small gardens." He added, "But I want everyone in the world to know this"—he indicated the wall, the tunnel, the plan of the electric fence looming before him. "This is the reality of occupation. Of colonization."

As we drove away from Omar's house, we went through the lands of the Kremisan monastery. The woods were idyllic. The trees grew without restraint, we could hear birdcalls, and the clearings of wild grass were strewn with fallen flowers. For a moment we forgot cameras, fences, walls. The moment passed; I was told the road would be closed in two weeks, and the wooded land annexed. Omar's children would have to make a forty-five minute trip to the school which was now five minutes away. If there was a medical emergency, what would Omar's family do?

* * *

Closed roads, checkpoints, annexed woods. Omar's reality of occupation, a reality with the face of a wall.

There is another wall, a wall in a poem Mahmoud Darwish wrote as if he knew Omar and his brothers and sisters and their children, and the wall that has come to them.

> A huge metal snake coils around us, swallowing up the little walls that separate our bedroom, bathroom, kitchen and living room... It twists and turns, a nightmare of cement segments reinforced with pliant metal, making it easy for it to move into the fragmented bits of land and beds of mint that are left to us. A snake eager to lay its eggs between our inhalations and exhalations so that we say for once, because we are nearly choking to death, 'We are the strangers.'[9]

Walls enclose the land, homes, people. Walls close the door to life as it was known, or as it is meant to be lived. Words have a little advantage over walls; they can vault walls. Like hope, the words people speak to each other, or to themselves, keep them going. They make an open book of words, these brave little foot soldiers of grandmothers, farmers, and poets. The same Darwish poem ends:

> We also see what lies behind the snake wall: the watchmen in the ghetto, frightened of what we're doing behind the little walls we still have left. We see them oiling their weapons to kill the gryphon they think is hiding in our pen coop. And we cannot help laughing.[10]

I had heard about the Darwish museum in Ramallah, and I went up a hilly road one afternoon in search of it. I stood outside the museum compound for a while, considering the town below. For me it was little more than a large village; but town or village, the place held its residents firmly inside a "Ramallah bubble." Leaving, and in some cases, coming back, was not exactly easy.

From my hilltop vantage point, I could see hills, settlements; winding roads down which taxis raced as if challenging the bubble; and buildings, more buildings coming up all over the place. I didn't see as many trees as I had expected to. I recalled what a Palestinian—a computer geek—told me as he drove me from Ramallah to Jerusalem. "Ramallah used to be a small hilly, tree-lined village," he said. "But power needs big buildings, not trees." He managed to be both sarcastic and wistful.

I turned away from the city and looked at the museum. From the outside, the building looked brand new, somewhat blank and bleached like an empty page that could be written on; a tabula rasa. An elegant young man in charge hastened to explain: the building has been designed to look like an open book. I went in with him to look at Darwish's life and words on display.

* * *

Mahmoud Darwish, often referred to as the Palestinian national poet, was born in 1941 in Al Birweh, a village in Galilee, under the British mandate in Palestine. When he was six, his world was turned upside down, and it never set itself right again. As the Israeli army occupied Birweh, Darwish and his family were forced to join the great exodus of refugees. They spent a year in Lebanon living on UN handouts. By the time they returned to their village in 1949, Israel had been created; their village was one of the hundreds of Palestinian villages that had been razed to the ground.

They were refugees again, infiltrators in their own land. Their return was "illegal"; they were given the status of "present-absent aliens."

Years later, Darwish recalled how his grandfather chose to live on a hill that overlooked his land. "Until he died he would watch [Jewish] immigrants from Yemen living in his place, which he was unable even to visit." The message of such an experience was: "You were not here. This was not Palestine."

Darwish described this identity in terms of a continuous "struggle between two memories." If his memories were real, his poetry had to challenge the Zionist tenet of "a land without a people for a people without a land." The result was, often, a strange contest within the poet. For instance, Darwish admired the work of the Hebrew poet Yehuda Amichai; but he also recognized that Amichai's poems were a challenge to him. Darwish said of Amichai, "He wants to use the landscape and history for his own benefit, based on my destroyed identity. So we have a competition: who is the owner of the language of this land? Who loves it more? Who writes it better?"

Darwish wrote of a state of siege in which anger simmers; but he also wrote,

Here on the slopes of hills, facing the dusk and the cannon of time
Close to the gardens of broken shadows,
We do what prisoners do,
And what the jobless do:
We cultivate hope.[11]

The "sense of abyss" Darwish wrote of could be transformed, he seemed to say, through political acts, and acts of imagination, into something more life affirming. In other words, there's siege, but there's also hope. There's loss, but there's also belonging.

Darwish was often called "the poet of the resistance"; but in the course of his life's work, he somehow managed to resist any neat or simplistic label. He wrote the Palestinian Declaration of Independence in 1988, and many poems of resistance that are an integral part of every Arab's consciousness. But he also allowed himself to grow into a poet who did not close his mind to other ways of seeing.

He said: "Poetry and beauty are always making peace. When you read something beautiful you find coexistence; it breaks walls down... I always humanize the other. I even humanized the Israeli soldier."[12] Just after the 1967 war, Darwish wrote a tender poem about an Israeli friend who decided to leave the country on his return from the front. The poem, "A Soldier Who Dreams of White Lilies," drew criticism from many admirers. But Darwish wrote that he would "continue to humanize even the enemy." This was the same Darwish who had not hesitated to write:

[To a killer] If you had contemplated the victim's face
And thought it through, you would have remembered
    your mother in the
Gas chamber, you would have been freed from the reason for the rifle
And you would have changed your mind: this is not the way
to find one's identity again.[13]

Darwish died in 2008. In 2002, he had, for some years, made the hills of Ramallah his home, close to where Raja Shehadeh still lives. (What kind of a home could it have been? "I have learned and dismantled all the words in order to draw from them a single word: *Home.*"[14])

There was curfew in Ramallah; Israeli tanks rolled down the narrow streets. One day, when curfew was lifted for five hours, Shehadeh interviewed Darwish. They spoke of many things, from Darwish's partiality for Mozart to the need to liberate Arabic poetry from older forms. When Shehadeh broached the subject of how the local landscape affected his poetry, Darwish replied:

> I find that the landscape is already written, and because
> it has been so fully described, I feel it is difficult to add
> to it. The poetic image has been realized geographically.
> My role as a contemporary poet is to liberate the natural
> landscape from the burden of those legends and ease the
> burden of history.[15]

10

ALMOST HOME

NAMING HOME, STAYING HOME: 1982, 2013

I have lived in Delhi for about thirty years now, and I should call it home.

This word, home. So easy to say, so casually said every day. Why then is home so hard to *see*, the way you see other places you visit for a week or two? Places I left behind twenty years back still come together to make sense, as if I can see them whole from above. The place of childhood thrives in my memory; it flourishes in my dreams. But the home that is, a single home in singular Delhi, resists a definitive biography.

Maybe too many people have written of the city's standing monuments, distracted by their hoary stories of brick, stone, and marble. Maybe too many people live in Delhi for years but do not think of themselves as dilliwallas and dilliwallis. Maybe it's this business of being a capital; the strain of being unity in diversity for all the nation, what boastful Indians and lazy foreign journalists like to call *the world's largest democracy*. Maybe the city knows, despite its formal salute to democracy in the police-permitted spectacles of protest at Jantar Mantar, that it has trouble keeping its promises.

There is an old story about this promise, though they did not refer to democracy in those days, but to its inner skin, justice. In the mid-eleventh century, a ruler called Anangpal set up two stone lions like gatekeepers of his palace in Delhi. A bell hung between the lions; citizens who sought justice could ring this bell. Once a crow struck this bell—we must assume by accident. But Anangpal decided that even the lowly crow was a citizen whose hunger must be taken seriously. A goat was killed. The crow could go back to being its bold self, picking meat from between the teeth of lions.

Hundreds of years later, Delhi has its crows, its blocks of stone, its pretend-lions. There are good days still, when the city seems a grand, ambitious palimpsest, with enough room for more Delhis. For more exiles and outsiders, refugees and migrants, rulers and ruled, Rajpath *and* Janpath. But most days the city leads its own life, like the more cruel face of nature. The people living in it wrestle endlessly with it, taming it into a semblance of home.

* * *

I must have first met Delhi through school textbooks, the dull sort that peddle official history. I heard my first vivid description of Delhi when I was about ten years old from a less reliable but more exciting source. My maternal grandfather lived in Coimbatore, and every summer his house was full of grand children visiting from other cities. All the children called him Doctor, though we rarely saw him practice medicine.

My grandfather once told us about a visit he had made to his daughter when she lived in Delhi. The summer was so hot there, he told us, that you could leave a raw *pappadum* on the road and it would cook itself to a crisp. Or you could fry an egg that way, since the natives of Delhi preferred eggs to pappadums. My grandfather watched us imagining this; he could see the wonder on our faces, and a touch of fear. Like the good storyteller he was, he paused, then told us what this heat did to people. "Delhi is a place," he told us, "where you have to be on guard all the time. You have to keep your eyes open. If you so much as blink, you get beaten up." He laughed with enjoyment and our fear evaporated. But I still promised myself I would never live in Delhi.

When I moved to Delhi in 1982, I did not see either pappadums or eggs on the roads. Besides, it was winter. I lived in South Delhi and worked across town on Asaf Ali Road, so I first got to know Delhi on the bus. Every morning I made my way to the Regal Cinema bus stop in Connaught Place. On the circuitous way, I looked through the bus window at endless blocks of government quarters—all architecturally categorized, and labeled with codes of letters and numbers. It was as if a bespectacled uncle spent all his time planning and classifying circles and avenues, or determining the caste of a building. He must have spent many hours agonizing over questions such as "Is this 'colony' D-1 or D-2, and should its SQ (or servants' quarters) have one window or no window?" Just when I was lulled by this stodgy love of order, the bus would take me past monumental Delhi; the larger-than-life ruins of Purana Qila, or elegant old tombs I knew nothing about.

Once I got off the bus at Regal, there was no more looking around. I had to push my way into a bus that was already full, find myself a square inch of space I didn't have to share with anyone. *Anyone* usually meant men.

There were, as others had found before me, many Delhis, far too many Delhis. But from the grandest building in the city's center to the *jhuggi-jopri* that make up unhappy shack-towns, everyone who breathes the capital air knows there is a god in Delhi.

I have now lived with (or despite) this god for many years, so I feel entitled to describe him in some detail.

The Delhi God likes monuments. This makes him partial to a particular sort of history, the kind we had to memorize as children, a stunningly long list of invaders, conquerors, dynasties, what each ruler did or didn't do.

He likes making official pronouncements, this god. He likes big buildings with many rooms in which these may be written. These rules, orders, notices, and procedures have many sections, subsections, clauses, exceptions, footnotes, often in fine print. This file-language abounds in words like "forthwith" and "hereto"; the language is called *sarkari*, or, sometimes, *gorement*. Over the years, these gorement rules, modifications forthwith and violations thereof, have used up so many reams of paper, filled up so many files, that they move very slowly, like crippled old men, from table to dusty table. Sometimes they don't move at all. They get eaten up by silverfish, or stolen by roving monkeys who sneak in through the window, grab a few files and shred them, reducing everyone's burden.

The Delhi God is definitely male, no Indian-tradition androgynous nonsense about him. He makes sure of an astonishing amount of free-floating testosterone in the city. I first met the Delhi God on the bus. As a lowly newcomer who had to take buses, I obviously did not deserve to meet the great man directly. But in true Delhi style, I met, through fellow commuters, his personal assistants and secretaries, his PAs and PSs in gorement-speak. Whether sly or aggressive, they rarely kept any part of their bodies to themselves. By the time I got to my office, a dingy basement near Turkman Gate, I would be furious and spoiling for a fight. The manuscripts I marked with a red pencil probably suffered unjust punishment day after day.

Home is like family. You can't bear it when others can see their warts and point them out. But you, you can see them all the time, you can make them bigger and uglier than they are. And because home is like family, you can take its better features for granted. Going up and down Asaf Ali Road in a bumpy cycle rickshaw between the two basements that housed sales and editorial, I would gaze at Turkman Gate, its graceful old arch, but I never found the time to explore further. Then one morning, Asaf Ali Road was cordoned off; the police were there in full force, and they refused to let me walk to my office. I looked down the street, empty of people and moving traffic. A long line of lorries stood like overweight ghosts; all their tires were flat. The police wouldn't tell me what had happened, and I was late for work. I decided to search for a rear entrance to the office building. Finally, after admiring Turkman Gate for months, I went into the city beyond and behind the gate.

* * *

Decades later, in 2013, I was back in the walled city to visit a woman called Naseem. She and I belong to the same women's organization. A friend and I walked down Bazar Chitli Qabar, searching for the turn into a swarm of lanes that would lead us to Pathak Ram Kishan Dass Gali.

It was a warm afternoon. The traffic—people, animals, cycle rickshaws—was bumper-to-bumper. I had barely escaped collision with a man carrying lethal-looking rods, when an irate rickshaw puller yelled at me to get out of his way. I jumped a few inches to the side, making sure I didn't land on garbage, or goods for sale, or tethered goats. It was the week before Bakri Id, and the old city had made room for what looked like the entire goat population of Delhi. Further down the street, a fragrance wafted out of a shop, settling delicately on the chaos in the street. It was the warm, loving smell of freshly baked bread. I stopped to admire the piles of loaves, inhaling deeply. A goat tethered nearby caught my eye; a little boy stood close to it. His hand cupped the goat's chin as he gazed tenderly into its eyes. The goat, untroubled by the brief and troubled path of love, looked smug.

We turned off the bazaar into a *gali*, a lane that grew narrower as it burrowed its way into clusters of shops, homes, hotels. Once upon a time these galis were wider. With encroaching construction and a growing desperation for space, the buildings are getting closer all the time. In some galis they seemed just a few inches apart, and this space was thickly curtained with garlands of wires. Pigeons, as rampant as the goats, perched confidently on the wires, watching the men at work on either side, tailoring, welding, dyeing, rolling out rotis.

* * *

Naseem lives deep in the fist of these galis. The house, or her part of what must once have been a house, is a small room with everything at floor level: mats, sheets, cushions, and pillows. Naseem lives here with her mother and her twenty-eight-year-old son. Every bit of space is used, but it looks neat, well cared for. There is one window, kept open; the door, too, remains open during our visit. The window grille, painted a fresh sapling green, bears a clothes-hanger with glass and plastic bangles. There is no sign of the beads she strings day after day, or the necklaces she makes on a piece-rate basis.

Naseem makes us comfortable with tea and biscuits, then sits down to talk.

The old city has always been Naseem's home. She went to school up to the eleventh standard a few streets away. I can easily imagine Naseem as a girl: her face must have been as it is now, open and unlined, a faint mole on one cheek, a stud sitting snugly on one nostril. Her head must have been covered; her father and uncle were strict about not letting her go anywhere outside the house alone. Then as now, the beads she strings were delivered to her house and the finished pieces picked up. Her father is dead, but the family—her brothers and sisters, assorted relatives, all live here still. Naseem's head is bare now. Her hair is a smooth black, except for a hint of henna at the hairline. She wears a dark kameez printed with pink flowers that seem to have their mouths wide open; they sit oddly with her soft, confidential manner.

Naseem did leave home once. She had a new home for fifteen days.

When she was seventeen, she got married. The marriage lasted one and a half months, but she actually lived with her husband for only fifteen days in his family home in Pilakura, past Ghaziabad. The fortnight was enough to get her pregnant. It was also enough to shape the course of the rest of her life.

Naseem studies the mat she is sitting on. Her voice is calm as she tells us what happened.

The trouble began on the wedding day. The bridegroom's family complained that the wedding food was not good enough; they felt they were not shown respect. When Naseem moved to her husband's house, there were more specific complaints: why had she not brought a TV or a fridge with her? Toward the end of that fortnight, she fell off the second floor while being beaten. Her leg was badly hurt. A few days later, her family brought her back to the Jama Masjid area. She went back to the life she knew—her parents and family and neighbors, her piece-rate work. Except now she had to support herself and the baby growing in her.

To begin with, she says, she "ate with her parents." But she saved up enough to pay the midwife a hundred rupees. As the years went by, she managed to see the child through school, a degree from nearby Zakir Husain College, then an architecture diploma. He has just got a job, but it is too soon to make any difference. Meanwhile, all his friends are married; some even have a couple of children. His marriage is getting delayed because Naseem's mother refuses to let her grandson bring a bride to this room. "He should get married," Naseem says, her face turning pensive for the first time. "But where will we go?"

My eyes travel to the only corner of the room that has furniture, her son's work corner. A steel *almirah* leans against the purple wall, to the side of a well-dusted table and chair. There is a small PC sitting on the table, an orange plastic bottle of water, and a container with three sharpened pencils. On the wall behind the table hang thumbtacked architectural plans and drawings.

"Everything I have, I have earned," Naseem says. "I don't want to leave this room, because I have a right to it." She lowers her voice, afraid her mother may return. "But my son must get married. We have to set up house somewhere else."

But she can't begin to imagine living anywhere else. Staying in this gali may be difficult, but she wants to remain in the area. It is safe, she "knows people in at least fifty houses." The place is filled with old relationships.

Her mother comes in, leaves again, having made sure it is only two of us and not a meeting. Naseem explains. Some years back, a woman from the neighborhood came to her house and asked her to join the local unit of a women's organization. Naseem paid up one rupee and became a member. Then she got curious and went to the local unit's office. "There were only women there, so it seemed all right to go," she adds. Gradually Naseem began to get involved. "At first I used to be scared of going to the police *thana* for a case," she says. "I would stand outside in the lane in my burqa—I still wear one if I have to go there—but I was afraid to go in." She smiles a little at her folly, but feels the need to explain this fear to us. "All I had done outside the home was go to school, come back; or go to relatives' houses on the street, come home. That's how I grew up, that's why I was scared of policemen."

She explains her role in the women's organization. "My job is to listen to those who have *dukh*. If a marriage is in trouble, we have to talk to everyone involved, find a solution. I ask the woman, Do you want to stay with your husband? I tell the woman about her rights, but we want people to stay together. I advise the man, tell him women need something, too... But if it comes to that, I go to the police thana, even the court."

Naseem's friend Naiyab drops in, and the conversation becomes general. "I don't have much time," Naiyab says as she sits down. "I have to go help with my nephew's wedding." With Id and an imminent wedding, the talk turns to *kheer*. Naseem tells us why her lane is popularly known as Kheer Wale Paathak. *Paathak* is the large container the kheer is cooked in; and once upon a time, her great grandfather used to make the milk pudding every day in this gali. "That was then," says Naseem, "but the name is still there." Naiyab discusses the best ways to thicken kheer.

We linger outside Naseem's house, saying goodbye in the tiny courtyard. The pink blooms of a *madhumalathi* creeper shade the courtyard, but the building coming up barely half a foot away looms above, cutting the sky into a stingy piece. In the neighborhood, they call these flats builders' flats. Their own one or two-room homes are houses, as if the memory of un-partitioned houses remains intact. All the other cities of Delhi seem irrelevant in the Jama Masjid *ilaka*. The area is just *Shahar*, or "city," as if it is the only city in the world worthy of the name. My friend suggests that those who live in Shahar consider the place superior because of its history of being protected by the royals. Naseem listens politely but says nothing. Home is where she has always been. It does not evoke pride; nor does it need explanation.

MAKING HOME: 1948, 2013

Not far from the walled city is a railway station. It is 1948. A nineteen-year-old, half boy, half man, gets off the train with his sister and brother. His home has become Pakistan; it is no longer home. Their parents are with them, but it is the two young men who lead the group as they make their way to the refugees' camp in Kingsway. They have already seen camp life across the freshly drawn border, in Amritsar, so this is not entirely new. Still, it is different: they have reached their destination, Delhi. They have two sets of clothes and hardly any cash.

The young man, Balraj Bahri Malhotra, is filled with energy, the sort that glides over fear and misery, races past the heartbreak of the hate and violence they have seen on their journey to Delhi; which they can probably still see, if they look underneath the surface of official camps, official relief and rehabilitation. All of Balraj's energy is directed at beginning a new life. Clerical jobs with the relief ministry; selling fountain pens; anything will do, as long as it is work and brings in some money. He hustles; so does his brother; they make new friends, look up distant relatives, seize every new opening, stretch it wide.

Sixty-five years later, Balraj Bahri tells me: "All I remember of that time was that I had no money, I only thought of how to live, get work—all that."

His father, who used to work in a bank, found it hard to get used to life in the barracks that made up Kingsway Camp. His mother found it easier. She had already learned what it was to "adjust" to a new home, having moved from her parents' Lahore house to a countrified small place, the new daughter-in-law of "modest but comfortable agriculturalists." Balraj and his brother had no time to think, or regret what they had left. With a combination of family contacts, new acquaintances from back home and from camp, hard work and good luck, the elder brother managed to get a shop in Lajpat Rai Market opposite the Red Fort. He got an agency for government publications. The father, who never adjusted himself to the new life in Delhi, was at the bookshop on time every morning.

Young Balraj sold pens in a relative's shop in Connaught Place, then for a congressman with a shop in Chandni Chowk. This man was beginning to acquire clout, and in 1951 he helped Balraj get a shop in Khan Market, which the government rebuilt for refugees in central Delhi. With his brother's example before him, Balraj, too, chose the book business. The shop in Khan Market, one-third of its present size, became Bahrisons Book Shop.

The shop stocked stationery, but Balraj knew nothing about books. In the three years of college he managed before partition, and later in his brother's shop, all he had seen were a few textbooks. Luckily he found a guide in the owner of a bookshop in

Connaught Place. Balraj walked every morning from Kingsway Camp to Khan Market, and sold stationery. He asked those who wanted books to write down what they wanted. Later in the day, he would rush to CP, and get his friend to help him get hold of these books. Slowly he made enough to buy a cycle.

"The early years were very difficult," Balraj Bahri tells me. His memory has no room for bitterness or self-pity. His voice sounds just like the four words that punctuate the conversation, *We had no choice*. Besides, it was in the refugee camp that he met a young woman who had made her own journey across the border with her mother and sister. She, too, had found work with the relief ministry. They got married, supported each other through the early years of living with the family in a camp. She got a house allotted in Netaji Nagar; he traded in his cycle for a scooter. Later, they built a house far from old Delhi and Kingsway Camp. Balraj got a car. Khan Market, too, changed, as if keeping pace with their fortunes. Today almost all the homes above the shops are gone; so are most of the refugee-managed shops, having given way to chic restaurants and stores. The place is prime property.

Delhi is home for the Bahri Malhotras. "My grandchildren are Delhi-ites. I have never gone back, even for a visit," Balraj Bahri says. "My son went to Pakistan once, but he only visited a couple of cities. He didn't go see the land which was ours."

He looks at the stacks of books around him, the tightly packed shelves of bestsellers and Booker Prize winners and children's books. "We have been lucky, I should say, compared to many others."

Balraj Bahri lets go of the past one more time. "If you forget the past, you are more comfortable. Those who don't forget find it hard."

Some refugee stories, at least, have a more or less happy ending. There are others, stories of refugees who would put the past behind them if they could finally find refuge in their adopted home. These refugees, with their burden of the wrong caste, or no contacts, or bad luck, or memories of violence, are not the only ones still trying to make home in Delhi.

* * *

Decades later, in 2013, the city rests on the shoulders of other cities invisible to its more respectable citizens. It would be hard for Delhi to run without being carried by these cities, places from where it gets its house cleaners, cooks, garbage collectors, rag pickers and recyclers, cart and tempo movers, small shopkeepers, mechanics, gardeners, electricians, plumbers, drivers, tailors, office peons, mall and call center employees. Together they make up some very large numbers, even by the impressive Indian standard for numbers. In these almost-hidden cities of Delhi are the homeless; those who make their homes in urban villages; and those who live, in government-tongue, in "notified slums" and "JJ clusters." Colonies of hutments. Jhuggi-jopri.

Unlike Mumbai, where slums are inescapable, Delhi is adept at keeping up appearances. If its slum colonies can't be hidden, the authorities can always curtain them with hoardings so visiting VIPs don't see them. This is what happened during the Commonwealth Games held in 2010. But mostly the city is able to wrap up these colonies and drop them into its crevices.

Kusumpur Pahari, for instance, is so cunningly tucked away that it can't be seen from the wide road that runs alongside. This road, named after Nelson Mandela, has malls selling Christian Dior and Louis Vuitton, and a seven-star hotel called The Grand. From Nelson Mandela Road, the stretch past the malls appears to be nothing but woods of scrubland. But this is where Kusumpur Pahari is. Maybe there is a shortcut through the woods; but to get there, I had to go all the way around, follow twists and turns off the upscale colony of Vasant Vihar. Just past the line of boards declaring a Delhi Metro work in progress, I found a lane, one of the two entries to Kusumpur Pahari. The name means city of flowers; a hilly city of flowers.

Soniya, an acquaintance from women's rallies, came down the lane to meet me. She has lived in Kusumpur for forty years.

We walked down the mud road past small grocery stores, butcher shops and carts selling vegetables; a Kanchan Beauty Parlor; a cell phone repair shop advertising *Ringtones! Wallpapers!* The innumerable little houses on either side are of plastered brick. Some look improvised, as if built in stages over the years. But they seem solid enough, painted in assertive colors. All the houses have rows of drums and jerry cans lined up like sentries. Or proof of residence, since everyone in Kusumpur has to store drinking water from the municipal tanker, water from the tube wells for other purposes.

The central street branches off into a maze of lanes. This is an entire city by itself, home to as many as a hundred thousand people.

We reached a large hall with an asbestos roof—the community center, where a nursery school session is in progress. The children were reciting multiplication tables aloud. When they saw Soniya, their volume went up a notch. *Dus paanch pachchas*, they called out with resounding certainty. Way at the back I saw a little boy sucking his thumb with furious concentration, his eyes fixed on an imaginary world where five times ten may make more than fifty. Soniya led me to the other end of the hall and we sat down to talk.

* * *

Soniya must be in her mid-fifties. Everything about her is neat and spartan, her black-framed glasses, the gray hair pulled back into a bun, the plain synthetic sari. She wears no jewelry except a plain band round her ring finger. She is dark and wiry-thin; I get a sense of simmering energy. She is an activist with the Mahila Samiti, but her work is not confined to women; she spends time in the school run by the Rotary Club in the community center; at night she goes back to the sewing machine, her source of income for many years.

Soniya grew up in Rangoon, where her father had a small ice factory. In 1969, when she was about fifteen, her father decided they would be safer in India. The family, parents and seven children, got into a free government ship, and in six days they were in Madras; a week later, they were back in the home of their ancestors in Uttar Pradesh. The government gave them a place to live in Faizabad. "But things were so bad," Soniya recalls, "I don't know how we lived." Her father was ill; Soniya and her mother weeded fields from morning to night and got one and a half rupees a day. They would eat only at night, making sure of leftovers for the little ones' lunch the next day.

I imagine Soniya, a girl bent over in the fields lit by an over-bright sun, taking a minute to straighten her back, stretch. Maybe she sees girls in school uniforms passing by, satchels on their backs. "I had nothing," says Soniya. "But I was always ready to talk to people." She asked around, sought out a "madam" who was the principal of a girls' college. The madam helped her join school. Soniya was much older than the other children; the bigger difference was that she had to work all day. She left school; but some years later, the madam helped her appear for the tenth standard exam privately. The madam also agreed that Soniya could cook food at home and sell it in the college canteen. The first day she felt strange; everyone was looking at her. But it was, says Soniya, "a question of feeding the stomach, feeding the household." Besides, there were only girls in the canteen.

Over the next four years, Soniya drew other members of her family into the work. The sales were good, the family's life improved; then the edifice came crumbling down. The madam left and the new madam changed their canteen arrangement. Soniya's family had to go back to finding work where they could. Her father grew frailer; her mother died of cancer. The family was a mess. And there was a new problem. For years, the villagers had gossiped about Soniya wanting to study, her working in the college canteen, then a nursery. Now they had something juicier: a matter of caste. A man who worked as an electrician and plumber in Delhi was visiting his sister in the village; he took to visiting Soniya. "The atmosphere in the village was bad," Soniya tells me. "There was a lot of caste-vaste, and they couldn't stand it that he was a Varma, friendly with me, a Yadav."

But Soniya was now a feisty twenty. When the neighbors called the police and her friend was beaten and locked up, she ran around for five terrible days looking for help, ignoring what people were saying. By the time he was brought to court—where he was released—she was so angry that she said in public, "I will marry him." Privately, she told Varma that marrying her would mean helping her family. "He agreed," Soniya says, "and kept his word." The pleasure of it is still able to light up her face. They were married, and she moved to Delhi. Because it was an intercaste marriage, she could not go to the village often. But when her younger sister's marriage was arranged, she made it a point to go. It was the first time the bride's sister went to check out the bridegroom in that village.

Like so many women in Kusumpur today, Soniya's Delhi life began in a *kothi*—one of the bungalows in Vasant Vihar. Living in the servants' quarters in a strange new city, she learned how to use a washing machine, how to lay the table with forks and knives, how to fold napkins. "I worked all day and I didn't earn much," Soniya remembers. "But I got one meal, I saw things I had never seen, and I learned a lot." Soniya smiles as she tells me, "My first Divali in Delhi, I got a sari with shiny little dots on it. It was the first time I had ever had a new sari."

About a year after her first child was born, Soniya knew her life had to change. "I will not work here," she told her husband. "I will not stay here either." And so, in 1979, he went to Kusumpur, which was quite empty then. He built a *jhuggi* with walls of bamboo. It was awful, Soniya remembers; no light or fan, no water; the baby became half her size in a week. "I was afraid my child would die." She retreated to another kothi in Vasant Vihar for a while, cooking for an old woman. But the jhuggi was there, waiting, calling her to a different life. They went back, made improvements. They learned to sleep out in the open so the nights were cooler. She learned tailoring so she could give up domestic work.

Soniya looks wistful as she shows me her younger self. This is what I see: hard work and the kindness of strangers; the seizing of a stray chance; a woman coming out of it all, fit to lead. This is the woman who now leads me away from the community center, through the streets of Kusumpur, to her house.

Kusumpur grew, she tells me, in the late eighties and early nineties. More and more migrants, mostly Hindus, came through the family network. Now there is no room for more. In fact, some are selling their houses—despite no papers—and moving out, especially since this talk of "resettlement" began. The Delhi Development Authority is conducting a survey. What they will do is not clear; they may try to move them to the outskirts of Delhi as they have done with other slums. But, says Soniya, they will resist. "If they want to build multistories here and relocate us, let them do it. But we are all agreed: resettle us here, or leave us alone. This is where our work is, this is home."

Home means they have voters' ID cards; ration cards; they have electricity and get bills; but they do not have papers—legal rights—over their houses. Home means the chance to fill up water from the tube well on alternate days; water from the tanker once a week. It also means, barring a few who have built a septic tank for themselves, living without a toilet. This is particularly hard on the women who have to go the "jungle" alone. And it means living with the liquor trade in the colony, something that will never die, says Soniya, as long as the police take their commission.

But Kusumpur is home. "Those fresh from the village have a problem at first," she says. "Then they leave the village behind, and become city people." She adds with quiet pride, "So many of our girls have studied, they will never work in kothis. They look smart, they work in offices, malls, call centers."

Home, for Soniya, also means activism. It is as much a part of her life as tailoring or cooking or filling up water in drums. "This place is full of NGOs," she says. "Our Mahila Samiti can't hand out things like NGOs; we run it with our own contributions. But our women's organization is strong because it stands by the people. It knows their problems well." She knows from experience how important the kindness of strangers is; but she also knows a home is not a house for one family, but a community.

On the street leading to her house, people waylay Soniya; some have questions for her, about ration cards, or a problem with a name left out of the DDA survey of the colony. Soniya answers every question patiently, then says goodbye to me, showing me the lane that leads out of the colony. "I will work with the Samiti as long as I live," she tells me as we part.

On my way back, I see a small clearing in the labyrinth of lanes and houses. In the center is a tree, roots hanging in the air. A cement circle has been built around the tree to make a meeting place. Bits of red cloth, some with a gold fringe, are tied to the tree's branches. They flutter like anonymous but festive petitions for a better life.

* * *

Sometimes it is enough to see what home means on the face of it: a house, a room; a shelter. In Kusumpur and other slums, they at least have a jhuggi, and their collective aspiration to seize a home from the city. But there is a Delhi where there are no huts, no tube wells or water tankers, no ration cards. And despite this Delhi being so full of nothing, there are people there, men, women, even children. They map their troubled lives onto the city as they survive day to day. The homeless know the knots and joints of the city, sleeping as they do on pavements, roads, railway platforms; or under bridges and flyovers; or in parks, handcarts, rickshaws, construction pipes; or around water tanks, temples, and markets. They know firsthand what it means to be destitute, to be people whom the city wants to disown, banish, lock up, or, at the very least, render invisible. Most know the fear of violence, from any quarter and at any time. Many know what it is to be preyed upon for sex. They know how easy it is to step across the line, give up on the wayward city and themselves, and turn to "solution" or other drugs, or petty crime. They also know what it is to be picked up by the police anytime, anywhere. Their homelessness is considered a crime; enforcing the statutes they violate by being homeless is more or less left to the police. This means that every now and then, the homeless can be picked up for "preventive detention" to promote "public peace." In the interest of public peace, they may languish in jail, or in remand homes as mean as the streets, till the system ejects them to the same nowhere place they came from.

A large number of the capital's homeless are children, part of the city's future. For now, in the present, they pick rags, push carts, work in street eateries, or sell pens or dusters or knick-knacks on the street. They find friends so they are not completely alone and unprotected. They learn to run away from policemen, just as so many of them have run away from a home that was no longer home. Sometimes a few find shelter for a while, in places run by well-meaning people. Even this temporary refuge means living with the fear that they may be "repatriated"—sent back to a home outgrown or disowned.

* * *

The room in which I wait for her is in an old building of red stone. It is a heritage building; it combines beauty and decay so well that I can't tell them apart.

A girl—let's call her Tara—arrives at the doorway, sees me waiting for her. She freezes. Every muscle of her body grows tense and alert. Her dark face closes up, blanking out everything.

Once she hears I have not come to take her back home, Tara's body unclenches. She comes in. But she remains guarded.

Three years back, the police brought Tara to this shelter from the railway station. Like the other children in the shelter, she goes to school. It may not be all that difficult to trace her home in Nepal, so there is every possibility that her days here are numbered. Every three months, the child-welfare people review her case. The young social worker in the shelter is on Tara's side. She says it is pointless sending her back because she may run away again, and the next time she may end up permanently on the streets.

Tara says she is thirteen years old, but she looks older. She wears faded blue jeans and a plain full-sleeved shirt. The shirt is missing the top button and is held in place with a safety pin. There's a watch and a thin steel bangle round one wrist; a bracelet of brown beads, and several yellow and red threads round the other. Her uncombed hair is held back with a rubber band, but a few strands have escaped so they frame her face like question marks.

When I ask if she lived in a city in Nepal, she agrees. When I ask her if she lived in a village, she doesn't disagree. But she is clear about what she has left behind. Her family is poor, but still, she used to go to school, or at least she did till the second standard. Then her mother left her father and married another man. The stepfather beat Tara; so did her mother. Of the three or four English words Tara uses in the conversation, the most striking one is "abuse." Her stepfather and mother pulled her out of school and made her work in their rag-picking business. None of their relatives wanted to have anything to do with them. It was, says Tara, because of the "shame of carrying rubbish around." Her elder sister got married and moved away; her elder brother went off, too, maybe to Delhi, she doesn't know.

How did she come to Delhi?

Tara has a hard time sitting still; her hands twist the threads round her wrist.

The story of how she got to Delhi, and what happened between her arrival and her coming to this shelter, varies. I get the sense she makes up different versions of herself for different people, different moments.

She tells me, at first, a story of bare bones. She came with her *mausi* to Delhi. Her aunt left her at the station. Some very good policemen brought her to the shelter. She likes it here, school is fine, everything is fine. She wants to study, her favorite subject is math.

It doesn't take long for a crack to appear in this story.

The other story, told at another point in our conversation: an "auntie" brought her to Delhi. The English word summons up another sort of aunt altogether. Tara was sent to work in a house. She didn't like it, so she was sent to another house. She says nothing about the two houses she worked in except that she had to "wash dishes, things like that," and that she didn't like it. She ran away and went back to the railway station. Again, she is silent about how long she was there, what she did there, why and how the police picked her up.

Does she have friends in the shelter? Or in school?

"No," she says, then "yes," shaking her head as if denying the yes.

She fusses with the threads round her wrist, reaches a compromise. "They are okay," she says, "there are many girls who talk to me, but I can't be talking to them all the time." She looks irritated. "We all have some secrets."

I agree. Does she tell her friends her secrets?

"No," she says, "and I don't want to hear theirs." It is hard to make out whether she disapproves of their stories, or their need to share them. Or whether she is afraid of trusting anyone who wants to be a special friend.

But Tara is still a child. Once she realizes I am not going to ask her questions about the home she ran away from, or the friends she claims and disowns in the same breath, she lets down her guard. She begins to enjoy, almost, the break from routine as she chats with a stranger who has no power over her. She loves to play, she tells me. She can play *kabbadi* and hide and seek, but what she likes best is badminton. These are the games she plays in the shelter.

What does she think of Delhi?

"It's full of people," she says, "too many people. And all of them are poor."

She doesn't like it. This is not home.

Where would she like to live, then?

"Shimla," she says.

Has she been there?

"No, but I have seen Shimla in pictures. In films," she says, laughing for the first time.

If she could have a home in Shimla, it would be a small empty house. Outside this house, there is nothing but snow, and a lone tree. The tree has no leaves, only branches. "The only light will be inside the house, and I will be there alone," she says. "I want to live in a place where I don't know anyone and nobody knows me."

And if she can't make it to Shimla? Where would she like to live?

"Delhi," she says, looking disappointed. Then she perks up. She will study, she says, then start a free school for children like herself.

She looks up at the wall behind me, her imagination going through it.

"There are many stories in my head," she tells me. "One day I will write the stories of each and every child I have met here. Then I will put these stories in all the libraries in Delhi."

NOTES

2. TWO CITIES OF VICTORY

1 Robert Sewell (1845–1925) was a collector and magistrate in Madras Presidency in colonial India. Like many of the civil servants-turned-Indologists of the time, he was a scholar in history. He was also in charge of the archeology department. His seminal work, *A Forgotten Empire: Vijayanagar; A Contribution to the History of India*, was published in 1900. He also translated two chronicles by the Portuguese envoy Domingo Paes and the Portuguese horse trader Fernão Nuniz, both eyewitnesses of Vijayanagar's glory. Their firsthand accounts formed the basis for many assumptions historians made about life in the imperial capital.

2 Muhammad Qasim Hindu Shah Astarabadi, known by the pen name Firishta. "Firishta" in Persian means "angel" or "one who is sent."

3 Translation of Basava's vachana by A.K. Ramanujan, *Speaking of Siva*, (London: Penguin Classics, 1973).

4 Clarence Lusane, *The Black History of the White House* (San Francisco: City Lights Open Media, 2011).

5 George Washington to John Francis Mercer, September 9, 1786. See http:// gwpapers.virginia.edu/articles/twohig_2.html#18.

6 Runaway Advertisement for Ona Judge, enslaved servant in George Washington's presidential household, by steward of the President's House. Frederick Kitt, in *The Pennsylvania Gazette*, May 24, 1796. See http://www. genealogywise.com/profiles/blogs/juneteenth-ona-judge-staines-a.

3. TODA CAFÉ BLUES

1 David G. Mandelbaum, "Culture Change among the Nilgiri Tribes," *American Anthropologist* (Berkeley: University of California Press, 1941).
2 Ibid., 22.
3 The origin of the name Udhagamandalam is obscure. The first mention of the place is as Wotokymund, in a letter dated March 1821 by an unknown correspondent to the *Madras Gazette*. In early times it was called Ottaikalmund. "Mund" is the Tamil word for a Toda village, and the first part may be a corruption of the local name for the central region of the Nilgiri Plateau.

4. MAPPING FREEDOM

1 Lalla Ded, http://www.koausa.org/Saints/LalDed/Vakhs1.html.
2 Agha Shahid Ali, "Farewell," *The Veiled Suite: The Collected Poems* (New Delhi: Penguin India, 2010), 177.
3 Report of the Fact Finding Team to Kashmir, *Four Months the Kashmir Valley Will Never Forget: An Enquiry into the Mass Uprising of 2010* (New Delhi: The Other Media, 2011), 7.
4 *Report of Independent People's Tribunal on Human Rights Violations in Kashmir* (New Delhi: Human Rights Law Network and Anhad, 2010).
5 Mehboob Jeelani, "The Other Kashmir Problem," *Caravan Magazine*, September 1, 2011, http://www.caravanmagazine.in/print/531#sthash. wQJvL4HI.dpuf.
6 Agha Shahid Ali, *The Veiled Suite*, 176–77.
7 Sheba Chhacchi, "Finding Face: Images of Women from the Kashmir Valley," in *Speaking Peace, Women's Voices from Kashmir*, ed. Urvashi Butalia (New Delhi: Kali for Women, 2002), 200.

5. SPEAKING IN HAIKU

1 Matsuo Bashō, *Haiku*, vol. 4, trans. R.H. Blyth (Dusseldorf: Nippon Shuppan Hanbai Deutschland GmbH, 1981), xxxv. See https://www.uwosh.edu/facstaff/ barnhill/es-244-basho/hokku.pdf.

2 Matsuo Bashō, *On Love and Barley: Haiku of Bashō*, trans. Lucien Stryk (Honolulu: University of Hawaii Press, 1985), 80.

3 Stephen Kohl, introduction to *The Master Haiku Poet, Matsuo Bashō*, by Makoto Ueda (New York: Twayne Publishers, Inc., 1970).

4 Trans. and ed. Robert Hass, *The Essential Haiku: Versions of Bashō, Buson, and Issa* (New York: Ecco, 1994), 40.

6. TRAILBLAZING IN ANDALUSIA

1 Ibn Zaydún,"Written from al-Zahra," trans. Christopher Middleton and Leticia Garza-Falcón, in *Andalusian Poems* (Boston: David R. Godine Publisher, Inc., 1994). Cited in Jerrilynn D. Dodds, María Rosa Menocal, and Abigail Krasner, "Thieves of Pleasure," *Humanities* 30, no. 2 (March–April 2009). See http://www.neh.gov/humanities/2009/marchapril/feature/thieves-pleasure.

2 For Wallada's, Hafsa's and Nazhūn's lives and poetry, see Arie Schippers, "The Role of Women in Medieval Andalusian Arabic Story-telling" in *Verse and the Fair Sex: Studies in Arabic Poetry and in the Representation of Women in Arabic Literature*, ed. Frederick de Jong (Utrecht: University of Utrecht Press, 1993), 139-52. See http://dare.uva.nl/document/2/80595.

3 Entry by Cristina Gonzalez in *Medieval Iberia, An Encyclopedia*, ed. E. Michael Gerli (New York: Routledge, 2002), 375.

4 Ibid.

5 Ibid.

6 Schippers, "The Role of Women," 146.

7 Averroës (Ibn Rushd), *Compendium of Medical Knowledge* (*Kitab al-Kulliyat fil-Tibb*), quoted in Caroline Stone, "Doctor, Philosopher, Renaissance Man," *Saudi Aramco World* 54, no. 3 (May–June 2003). See www.fordham.edu/halsall/source/1190Averroës.html.

8 Ibn Zaydún, "The Nuniyya," trans. Michael Sells, in *The Cambridge History of Arabic Literature: The Literature of al-Andalus*, eds. María Rosa Menocal, Raymond P. Scheindlin, and Michael Sells (Cambridge: Cambridge University Press, 2000).

7. LOOKING FOR A NATION, LOOKING AT THE NATION

1 Anonymous, "French Algeria," *Quarterly Review* 99 (1856), quoted in Thomas Rid, "Razzia: A Turning Point in Modern Strategy," *Terrorism and Political Violence* (New York: Routledge, 2009).

2 Alexis de Tocqueville, "Rapports sur l'Algérie," (1853) *Oeuvres completes* t. VI, vol. i, ed. J.P. Mayer (Paris: Gallimard, 1954), quoted in Olivier Le Cour Grandmaison, "Torture in Algeria: Past Acts that Haunt France, Liberty, Equality and colony," trans. Harry Forster, *Le Monde diplomatique*, June 2001, http://mondediplo.com/2001/06/11torture2.

3 *Lettres choisies, souvenirs (1814–1859)*, eds. Françoise Mélonio and Laurence Guellec, (Paris: Gallimard, 2003), quoted in John W.P. Veuglers, "Tocqueville on the conquest and colonization of Algeria," *Journal of Classical Sociology* 10, no. 4 (November 2010), 339, http://jcs.sagepub.com/content/10/4/339.

4 "Visite a l'un des tribunaux civils de Quebec," *Oeuvres completes* t. V, vol. i., ed. Mayer (1957), quoted in Veuglers, "Tocqueville on the conquest and colonization of Algeria."

5 Letter to Henry Reeves on September 22, 1857, Alexis de Tocqueville, *Oeuvres completes* t. VI, vol. i, ed. Mayer, 236, quoted in Hugh Brogan, *Alexis de Tocqueville: Prophet of Democracy in the Age of Revolution* (London: Profile Books, 2006).

6 *Oeuvres completes* t. III, vol. iii, ed. Mayer (1962), quoted in Melvin Richter, "Tocqueville on Algeria," *The Review of Politics* 25, no. 3 (July 1963).

7 Alexis de Tocqueville, "Lettre sur l'Algerie" (1837), in *Sur l'Algerie*, ed. Seloua Luste Boulbina (Paris: Flammarion, 2003), quoted in Veuglers, "Tocqueville on the conquest."

8 Ibid., 346.

9 Tocqueville, "Travail sur l'Algerie," (1841), in *Sur l'Algerie*, ed. S.L. Boulbina, quoted in Veuglers, "Tocqueville on the conquest."

10 Grandmaison, "Torture in Algeria."

11 Raymond F. Betts, *Assimilation and Association in French Colonial Theory, 1890–1914* (Lincoln: University of Nebraska Press, 2005).

12 Frantz Fanon, "The Problem of the Colonized," in *Toward the African Revolution: Political Essays*, trans. Haakon Chevalier (New York: Grove Press, 1964), 15.

13 Fanon, trans. Haakon Chevalier, "Letter to a Frenchman," in *Toward the African Revolution*, 49.

14 Ibid., 50.

15 Djamila Amrane, Farida Abu-Haidar, "Women and Politics in Algeria from the War of Independence to Our Day," *Research in African Literatures* 30, no. 3 (Fall 1999), 62–77.

16 Bouthina Shaaban, *Both Right and Left Handed: Arab Women Talk About Their Lives* (Bloomington: Indiana University Press, 1988), 196, quoted in Caroline Rohloff, "Reality and Representation of Algerian Women: The Complex Dynamic of Heroines and Repressed Women," (Illinois Wesleyan University, Digital Commons@IWU, 2012), 9.

17 *Gender and National Identity: Women and Politics in Muslim Societies*, ed. Valentine Moghadam, (London: Zed Books, 1994), 47, quoted in Rohloff, "Reality and Representation of Algerian Women."

18 Danièle Djamila Amrane-Minne, "Women at War," trans. Alistair Clarke, *Interventions* 9, no. 3 (2007), 344, quoted in Rohloff, "Reality and Representation of Algerian Women," 9.

19 Ibid.

20 Ibid.

21 Ibid.

22 Frantz Fanon, "Concerning a Plea," *Towards the African Revolution*, 66.

23 Marnia Lazreg, *Torture and the Twilight of Empire: From Algiers to Baghdad*, (Princeton: Princeton University Press, 2008), 3.

24 Quote from Djamila Boupacha in Simone de Beauvoir and Gisele Halimi, *Djamila Boupacha* (Paris: Gallimard, 1962), quoted in Lazreg, 145.

25 Natalya Vince, "Colonial and Post-Colonial Identities: Women Veterans of the 'Battle of Algiers'," *French History and Civilization* 2 (2009), 153, http://eprints.port.ac.uk/5050/1/Vince_Final_Version.pdf.

26 The 1984 Family Code, based on a conservative interpretation of *sharia* law, legally obliged women to obey their husbands, and reduced the grounds on which women could demand divorce. In 2005, the government initiated a partial reform of the 1984 Family Code, or "scandalous law."

27 Interview with Zohra Drif in 2005, quoted in Vince, "Colonial and Post-Colonial Identities," 162.

28 http://news.bbc.co.uk/2/hi/africa/4926128.stm.

29 Quoted in Vince, "Colonial and Post-Colonial Identities," 158.

30 Ibid.

31 Interview with David Macey on Fanon, Foucault and Race by Simon Dawes, January 5, 2011, http://theoryculturesociety.blogspot.in/2011_01_02_archive. html.

8. BITTERSWEET DANISH

1 Holger Drachmann, "Sangenes Bog," *Samlede Poetiske Skrifter* 8 (Copenhagen: Gyldendalske Boghandel, 1908), 492, quoted in Martin Zerlang, "Danish Orientalism," *Current Writing: Text and Reception in Southern Africa* 18, no. 2 (2006).

2 Epigraph of Hans Christian Andersen, *A Poet's Bazaar*, in Zerlang, "Danish Orientalism," 121.

3 Georg Brandes, ibid.

4 Elisabeth Oxfeldt, *Nordic Orientalism: Paris and the Cosmopolitan Imagination 1800–1900* (Copenhagen: Museum Tusculanum Press, 2005).

5 Peter Hervik, "The Danish Muhammad Cartoon Conflict," *Current Themes in IMER Research* 13 (2012), www.mah.se/muep.

6 Ibid.

7 Kiku Day, "Denmark's New Values," *Guardian*, February 15, 2006, http://www. guardian.co.uk/world/2006/feb/15/muhammadcartoons.comment.

8 Signe Toft, "A-manden, Amin og antropologen. Et essay om Jyllands-Postens fremstillinger af 'fremmede' og om læsernes opfattelser af forskellighed," in *Den generende forskellighed*, ed Peter Hervik (Copenhagen: Hans Reitzels Forlag, 1999) cited in Hervik, "The Danish Muhammad Cartoon Conflict."

9 Ibid., 31.

10 Morten Langager, "Borgerlige skræmte over ny prognose," *Morgenavisen Jyllands-Posten*, July 16, 2001, quoted in Hervik, "The Danish Muhammad Cartoon Conflict."

11 Ibid., 31.

12 Ibid., 83.

13 Joshua Keating, "The countries that won't let you name your kid something ridiculous," *Foreign Policy* blog, January 4, 2013, http://foreignpolicy.com/2013/01/04/the-countries-that-wont-let-you-name-your-kid-something-ridiculous/.

9. SEEING PALESTINE

1   William M. Thomson, *The Land and the Book* (New York: Harper & Brothers, 1860), quoted in Hilton Obenzinger, "Holy Land Travel and the American Covenant: 19th Century Palestine in the Settler-Colonial Imagination," *Jerusalem Quarterly* 17 (February 2003), 17, http://www.jerusalemquarterly.org/images/ArticlesPdf/17_holyland.pdf.

2   *Excerpts from Edward Robinson, Biblical Researches in Palestine, Mount Sinai and Arabia Petrae: A journal of travels in the year 1838* (Boston: Crocker & Brewster, 1841), http://www.getty.edu/art/exhibitions/biblical_lands/.

3   Quoted in Hilton Obenzinger, "Herman Melville Returns to Jerusalem," *Jerusalem Quarterly* 43 (2010), http://www.jerusalemquarterly.org/ViewArticle.aspx?id=352.

4   "In Search of Biblical Lands: From Jerusalem to Jordan in Nineteenth-century Photography," The J. Paul Getty Museum, http://www.getty.edu/art/exhibitions/biblical_lands/.

5   http://www.eretzyisroel.org/~peters/depopulated.html.

6   Edward W. Said, *The Politics of Dispossession, The Struggle for Palestinian Self-Determination 1969–1994* (New York: Vintage, 1995), 108–9.

7   Judea and Samaria are the biblical names for the general areas south and north of Jerusalem (respectively). Historically, they include substantial portions of pre-1967 Israel, but not the Jordan Valley or the Benyamina district (both within the West Bank). For political purposes, and despite the geographical imprecision involved, the annexationist camp in Israel prefers to refer to the area between the green line and the Jordan River not as the West Bank, but as Judea and Samaria. Ian S. Lustick, *For the Land and the Lord: The Evolution of Gush Emunim* (New York: The Council on Foreign Relations, 1988), http://www.sas.upenn.edu/penncip/lustick/lustick13.html#txt4.

8   http://www.stopthewall.org/isolated-home-hani-amer.

9   Mahmoud Darwish, "The Wall," trans. Catherine Cobham, in *A River Dies of Thirst: Journals* (New York: Archipelago Books, 2009), 37.

10 Ibid.

11 Mahmoud Darwish, "Under Siege," trans. Marjolijn De Jager, from Adab.com Arabic Poetry, http://www.adab.com/en.

12 Maya Jaggi, "Profile of Mahmoud Darwish," *Guardian*, June 13, 14, http://www.theguardian.com/books/15/jun/16/featuresreviews.guardianreview17.

18 Darwish, "Under Siege," trans. De Jager.

19 Mahmoud Darwish, "I Belong There," in *Unfortunately, It Was Paradise, Selected Poems*, trans. Munir Akash and Carolyn Forché (Berkeley and Los Angeles: University of California Press, 2003), 7.

20 Raja Shehadeh, "Mahmoud Darwish," *BOMB* 81 (Fall 2002), http://bombsite. com/issues/81/articles/2520.

ACKNOWLEDGMENTS

A few parts of these essays were published in earlier versions in newspapers, magazines, and books as follows: "Seven Cities and Anycity" in *Storie*, Leconte Editore, Rome, 2003; "Two Cities of Victory" in *Merian*, Hamburg, 1997, and the *Telegraph*, Kolkata, 2004; 'Toda Café Blues" in the *Telegraph*, Kolkata, 2008, and *Moving Worlds*, 2010; "Trailblazing in Andalusia" and "Speaking in Haiku" in the *Telegraph*, Kolkata, 2009 and 2010 respectively; "Mapping Freedom" in Newsclick.in, 2012; and "Seeing Palestine" in *Frontline*, Chennai and Newsclick.in, 2013, and Githa Hariharan (ed.), *From India to Palestine: Essays in Solidarity*, LeftWord Books, 2014. The quotation at the beginning of this book is from *Invisible Cities* by Italo Calvino, published by Vintage and reprinted by permission of the Random House Group Ltd.

This book began with a work of art. When I first saw Ellen Driscoll's *The View from Here*, the images of travel and traveler, gazer and gazed upon, spoke to me. So did the title, encouraging me to write essays which describe the view from an Indian "here." I am grateful for Ellen's work, our discussions over the years, and for *The View from Here* as a guiding spirit to this book. For more on Ellen Driscoll's work, see http://ellendriscoll.net/.

I thank Valerie Borchardt and Georges Borchardt for their belief in my work and their support.

Many friends read this or that essay and gave me thoughtful comments. Of these, I must single out Anjali Singh, V.K. Karthika, Raja Shehadeh, Sahba Husain, Alan Cheuse, Lotta Strandberg, Aamer Hussein, and Ritu Menon for special thanks. Prabir Purkayastha played the essential roles of listening post and non-literary critic. As for my sons, Nishad Bailey and Rishab Bailey, I am happy to thank them always, even when they may not deserve it.

Most of all, I thank all those who shared the stories they know, including their own, with such generosity and patience.

ABOUT THE AUTHOR

Born in Coimbatore, India, GITHA HARIHARAN grew up in Bombay and Manila. She was educated in those two cities and later in the United States. She has worked as a staff writer for WNET-Channel 13 in New York, an editor for Orient Longman, a freelance professional editor for a range of academic institutions and foundations, and visiting professor at a number of international universities. Her first novel, *The Thousand Faces of Night* (1992) won the Commonwealth Writers' Prize for best first book in 1993. Her other novels include *The Ghosts of Vasu Master* (1994), *When Dreams Travel* (1999), *In Times of Siege* (2003), and *Fugitive Histories* (2009). She has also published a highly acclaimed short story collection, *The Art of Dying*, and a book of stories for children, *The Winning Team*. Her essays and fiction have also been included in anthologies such as Salman Rushdie's *Mirrorwork: 50 Years of Indian Writing 1947–1997*. She lives in New Delhi.

RESTLESS BOOKS is an independent publisher for readers and writers in search of new destinations, experiences, and perspectives. From Asia to the Americas, from Tehran to Tel Aviv, we deliver stories of discovery, adventure, dislocation, and transformation.

Our readers are passionate about other cultures and other languages. Restless is committed to bringing out the best of international literature—fiction, journalism, memoirs, poetry, travel writing, illustrated books, and more—that reflects the restlessness of our multiform lives.